CADMUS
BOOKS

THE FABULOUS WORLD OF OPERA

by

Dorothy and Joseph Samachson

Illustrated with photographs

To hear music at its most spectacular, listen to opera. For many years it was so expensive that it was heard only by monarchs. The wealth of princes was judged by the opera houses they maintained. Today we hear magnificent music on the radio or produced on television. Even with the wide screen, it is impossible to get the impact of the complete opera, unless you see it on stage. With recordings and other methods of reproduction, arias are familiar to millions of opera-lovers. It is important to learn more about it, and this book gives you an idea of how opera has grown and developed since the seventeenth century. You will go behind the scenes and see what the librettists, conductors, choreographers, designers as well as the singers and directors do in the development of this dramatic art.

⚜

Classification and Dewey Decimal: Music (782.1)

About the Authors:

DOROTHY and JOSEPH SAMACHSON are a husband-and-wife writing team with highly diversified talents. Mrs. Samachson is a professional pianist and it is she who does most of the research, interviewing and selection of pictures. Dr. Joseph Samachson, who received his Ph.D. from Yale University, has been head of a hospital chemical laboratory. His writing of murder mysteries, science fiction and scientific articles are a spare-time activity. The Samachsons have two grown children and live in a suburb of Chicago.

Above: *George London, American singer, appears as Boris Godunov at the Bolshoi Theatre in Moscow.* Below: *A scene from* Das Rheingold *about 1913 at the Metropolitan Opera House. Obviously, scenery, make-up, costumes, and staging have changed considerably since.*

The Fabulous World of OPERA

DOROTHY & JOSEPH SAMACHSON

Illustrated with photographs

1966 FIRST CADMUS EDITION
THIS SPECIAL EDITION IS PUBLISHED BY ARRANGEMENT WITH
THE PUBLISHERS OF THE REGULAR EDITION
RAND McNALLY & COMPANY
BY
E. M. HALE AND COMPANY
EAU CLAIRE, WISCONSIN

To Michael, Miriam, and David

 Printed in U.S.A.
Library of Congress Catalog Card Number: 62-13169
First printing, 1962
Second printing, 1966

contents

illustrations

introduction

TO ATTEND THE OPERA is to listen to music at its most spectacular. Opera is so complex, so many-sided, and so expensive a form of art that in the days of absolute monarchies, the wealth and power of princes were judged by the opera houses they maintained. Every court with any pretense to social standing had its own composers and designers, its own instrumentalists and singers, all paid from the treasury of the local ruler. The San Carlo Opera House in Naples, for example, was built in 1737 by order of Charles III. Naples at that time was renowned for its opera, and the new royal theatre matched the music in magnificence, adding luster to the king's name. The Berlin Court Opera, dating from an even earlier era, for more than two hundred years enjoyed the patronage of the kings of Prussia.

Because of this princely support, in many places only the royal family and members of the nobility could enjoy the pleasures of opera. Now, of course, the situation is different. For many months of the year, opera is available to hundreds of thousands of people in many countries. Millions more have grown to know and love opera, and have their own favorites from listening to broadcasts and to recordings.

And yet, to millions of others, opera remains something foreign, a spectacle that they identify chiefly with society and snobbery—a dull spectacle at that, for the bored individuals they see at the opera in many movies, for example, usually go only to show themselves in jewels and fine clothes, and are so busy looking around for famous or notorious people that they pay no attention to the music.

In parts of Europe, operas are televised rather frequently. In the United States, on the other hand, few operas have appeared on TV or on the movie screen, but these few have given large audiences a chance to correct mistaken impressions, and to get a glimpse of what drama with music can be. A glimpse is not enough, however, for even the largest television or movie screen lacks the dimensions of the opera stage, and loses something of both the color and the sound of a live performance.

Those who have had their appetites whetted by television, records, or movies are fortunate if they have the opportunity to see a full stage production. When well done, opera is one of the most alluring forms of entertainment ever invented, its visual and emotional excitement keeping an audience entranced from beginning to end. In it you have the world of make-believe at its most magical, the beautiful voices conspiring with some of the greatest music ever written to sweep you into a story of powerful human passions.

That is why there have been times and places when opera has driven spoken drama from the theatre, when even the plays of Shakespeare could not be put upon the stage without being cut, fitted to music, and produced as synthetic operas. The quality of these spectaculars was unfortunately low, and they did not survive, but there was nothing wrong with the idea of setting Shakespeare's plays to music. Later on, for example, Verdi*

* The birth and death dates of all composers mentioned in the book appear in the index.

made a genuine opera of *Othello,* and this musical masterpiece remains very high in the esteem of critics and public.

Most of us are familiar with a number of operas without realizing that they are operas at all. We usually call them musical comedies, but *West Side Story, Oklahoma!, My Fair Lady,* and *Finian's Rainbow* are as much operas as Monteverdi's *Orfeo* (*Orpheus*), first performed in 1607, or Bizet's *Carmen,* produced in 1875.

Let us admit, rather, that they are not traditional opera. But why must opera be limited to the traditional? The history of opera is in fact the story of a number of musical and dramatic revolutions. In the past many have said that the new works being written for the opera stage were not only ugly and uninteresting, but were not really operas at all. Often, however, the very works that aroused the most opposition when they were first presented have been absorbed into the dramatic repertory and have become part of a new tradition.

People enjoy opera for different reasons: some because they like the music; others because they enjoy the singing, or because they are moved by the dramatic action and by their feeling for the characters. Some are fortunate enough to enjoy opera in all its aspects. Music is the most important element in opera, but it is not the only element. An opera is intended to move an audience to tears and laughter. When Puccini wrote *Madama Butterfly,* * he would have considered his heroine's arias a failure if they had left his audience dry-eyed. And when Mozart wrote comic arias for *Le Nozze di Figaro* (*The Marriage of Figaro*) he was not merely creating beauty; he was writing music to laugh with.

* Opera names are usually given in the original language when first mentioned; all further references are in English. There are a few exceptions, such as *The Bartered Bride* and *Der Freischütz,* when the best-known title is used regardless of language.

Mozart's music not only helps to create the characters we see on stage; it exhibits a humor of its own in its comments on the action. Music, story, and stage action work together to evoke the emotional effect in those who watch and listen.

The more familiar one becomes with opera, the more one can find to enjoy. That is one reason for learning more about it. Another reason, of course, is that opera is worth knowing about for its own sake. For in opera at its best we find the elements of several different arts—painting, sculpture, literature, and music —fused into one fascinating form.

Opera was not born accidentally. It was deliberately created, and one of the most interesting aspects of its creation is the fact that its inventors, as they may be called, had a mistaken idea of what they were doing. They did not think that they were producing anything new at all. They were under the impression that they were merely reviving a form of drama that had died nearly two thousand years before.

To get an idea of the ways in which opera has grown and developed, let us go back to see what the stage looked like just before the beginning of the seventeenth century, when the new form of dramatic art first appeared.

the growth of opera 1

At the end of the sixteenth century, the people of Italy were acquainted with different forms of entertainment in which music and drama were combined. They knew, to begin with, the *commedia dell' arte,* the lively and frequently vulgar improvised comedy of the market place, performed by troupes of strolling actors. This was ordinarily spoken, but after a comic scene there might be a ribald song, which very likely had nothing to do with the theme of the comedy as a whole.

On a more lofty level, they could see and hear the so-called madrigal comedy. A madrigal was a song written for a number of different voices. As each singer had both his own words and his own melody, the result when four people sang together may have been musically pleasing, but the meaning of the words could not have been easy to grasp. Nor was a series of such madrigals effective in carrying on dramatic action.

For the upper classes there was the *pastorale,* a dramatic poem about the sorrows and delights of shepherds and shepherdesses, nymphs and goddesses. Some of these pastorales were elaborately produced and became popular among the nobility. As they were sometimes serious and stuffy, the audiences began to find relief in the *intermedio,* a musical number given as a prologue to the main work, or sandwiched in between the acts. The music of

Two stock characters of the commedia del arte.

the *intermedio* became more and more welcome as time went on, and retained its popularity through the seventeenth century.

None of these forms of amusement or art satisfied the *Camerata* or *Chamber Group,* members or associates of the Italian nobility who met in the palaces of different noblemen. What these amateurs wanted was a return in music and drama to the ideas and ideals of the ancient Greeks. The Greeks had long loomed in the minds of medieval scholars as almost mythical giants, and attempts to revive their greatness had been made from at least the thirteenth century on. In drama the attempt was made more difficult by the fact that no one knew exactly how the ancient Greek plays had been performed. It was believed that in Greek drama the actors chanted or declaimed poetry against what must have been a very skimpy musical background. The ancient Greek musicians did not play harmonies in our sense of the word and their musical instruments were few and primitive, so that without question the poetry was of greater importance than the music.

The Greeks emphasized the poetry, not necessarily from choice, but because of the undeveloped nature of their music. The members of the *Camerata* saw in this emphasis a real virtue. They too would stress the greatness of the poetry. The poets among them apparently took it for granted that they would write great poetry, as the Greek dramatists of two thousand years before had done, and the composers, not being sure of their own abilities, agreed modestly that the music would be of secondary interest.

In all the theories of the *Camerata,* the importance of the words was stressed. First came the negative requirement that the music must not prevent the words from being understood, as it prevented them from being understood in the madrigal. On the positive side, it must follow the accents and rhythms of the words. And, finally, it appeared to the theorists that it would be a good idea if the composer not only depicted in sound what was being said in poetic imagery, but interpreted the feeling as well.

The first crude model of the new invention was *Dafne,* the music of which was composed in 1594 by Jacopo Peri to a poem by Ottavio Rinuccini. *Dafne* was performed in 1597, but the music was then lost and only two fragments survive. *Euridice,* written in 1600 by the same poet and composer, was performed the same year, and its music has come down to us.

The "New Music," as the early operatic works were called, was successful enough to be imitated in the next few years all over Italy. It was dignified because the poetic text was serious, all comedy being excluded, and the music obeyed the theoretical requirements by not getting in the way.

In Peri's *Euridice,* for example, there was no overture, nor did the instruments play more than a few brief connecting passages

Jacopo Peri, member of the Camerata, and composer of Euridice, *the first opera that has survived. He is shown in costume for the role of Orfeo, at the wedding of Henry IV of France to Maria de Medici in Florence, 1600.*

between scenes. Usually, in these early operas, no more than four instruments accompanied the voices. Listening to the words alone, you heard poetry. Listening to the music alone, you heard sounds that hardly deserved the name of melody. The effect was quite different from that of modern opera.

This "New Music" was better than performances of the same plays without any music at all, but at the same time the lack of musical variety often became monotonous.

In the next few years, however, opera was further developed by Claudio Monteverdi, a composer of genius. No mere theorist, but a professional musician who could write beautiful melodies, Monteverdi, in his very first opera, *Orpheus,* performed at Mantua in 1607, did things differently. To create atmosphere that would put his audience in the right mood before ever a word was spoken, Monteverdi wrote an overture. He added instruments to the tiny original orchestra and gave these instruments more important parts to play. And he forgot all the nonsensical theories about making the music secondary to the poetry.

He wrote songs in which words and music united to create an intense emotional effect. He used all the resources of melody, harmony, and instrumentation then known, to move his audiences, and when the results didn't satisfy him, he created new effects. He introduced the pizzicato—the plucking of strings—and the tremolo—the rapid alternation of two notes—to generate an atmosphere of excitement. For his opera, *Arianna,* he composed an aria known as "Arianna's Lament" which moved audiences all over Italy to tears. Previous composers of opera had moved them to little beyond the mildest of emotions.

None of these early operas got completely away from the Greeks. If not based on the theories of Greek drama, they were at least based on Greek myths. *Orpheus* and *Eurydice* are in fact the same story, which tells how Orpheus, the greatest of musicians, went down to Hades to rescue his bride, Eurydice, from the kingdom of the dead. In the original Greek myth he was successful, but lost Eurydice again because he did not obey the

Claudio Monteverdi

gods. Patrons of the early operas did not like unhappy endings, and to please them the composers permitted Orpheus to keep his Eurydice.

In Florence, in Mantua, and in Rome, where it was also performed, the new Florentine theatrical style, as opera began to be called, was meant for the court alone, and retained its dignified, serious character. In 1637, however, the first opera house was opened in Venice, to be followed by a number of others. Here opera soon became the rage. This city of 125,000 people, a population less than that of many a moderate-sized American city, supported at one time six opera troupes, who gave performances in any one of seventeen theatres, and had seasons lasting from twelve to thirty weeks. From an aristocratic entertainment, opera became the favored public entertainment of rich Venetians.

The changes were striking. Gone was the emphasis on lofty poetry, gone was the well-constructed plot. The chorus, beloved of the Greeks and their Florentine imitators, disappeared for a time almost completely. The Venetians preferred a good rousing solo to the dignified chants of the gloomy commentators on the action. What was lost in plot construction was made up by a gain in dramatic effect. Contrast was provided by from fifteen to twenty scenes in every act, while visual excitement was taken care of by devils, gods, sieges, shipwrecks, battles, fireworks, explosions, and all the elaborate stage devices developed originally by medieval mechanicians for the miracle and mystery plays of the late Middle Ages.

No longer was the music subordinate to the poetry. Instead, everything was subordinate to the music, or rather to one special form of it: the vocal solo. The *aria,* or solo air, became the most important musical form. And along with the importance of the song went the importance of the singer. The soprano, male and female, soon dominated opera.

As early as 1607, *Orpheus* had introduced the first *castrato* or male soprano (or contralto). These men with women's voices had marvelous vocal technique, and composers wrote arias that were dazzling and difficult, if not musically worthwhile, merely as display pieces for them. If the composer refused to write the kind of music the singer demanded, the latter could always modify his part in actual performance, adding trills, holding notes for as long as his breath held out, racing up and down the scale to display his vocal agility. So long as the audience roared its approval, who cared what became of the story?

In these changes, opera lost much of its poetry and sense of plot, as well as some of its good taste, and its appeal to the more refined feelings of its audiences. Its frequent cheapness and vulgarity were plain to every intelligent person, and by its emphasis on vocal display it offended those who genuinely liked music. What it gained, however, eventually more than compensated for what it lost. It acquired a sense of life, of being part of the hopes and fears of actual beings.

It still dealt largely with mythical subjects: Orpheus, Hercules, Greek gods and goddesses. But its characters were no longer as shadowy as they had been in the first *Eurydice*. From the time of Monteverdi's *Orpheus* on, they had become more and more human. Monteverdi continued to write operas, and his works of 1641 and 1642, created for the Venetian public, show that the requirements of his new audience had affected him. He created livelier operas, and could not help making concessions to the demands of the singers. But he had not lost his genius.

With the relaxation of the old aristocratic standards, comic scenes had been inserted into serious operas. Comic opera as such, or *"opera buffa,"* as it was called (see glossary), grew naturally out of these scenes and out of the existence of the *commedia dell' arte*. The librettos (or texts) for the first two comic operas were written by Giulio Rospigliosi, who later, in 1667, became Pope Clement IX. His first comedy *Chi Soffre, Speri (Who Suffers May Hope)* was performed in Rome in 1639. His *Dal Male il Bene (Good for Evil)* was performed in 1654.

The entire spirit of operatic music slowly changed. The early operas had been written in the old *modes*—according to melodic patterns which had come down to the end of the sixteenth century, with little alteration, from the days of the ancient Greeks. They had an archaic sound, strongly suggestive to our ears of church music. Because the music followed the irregular rhythm of the words, it had no strongly marked beat. And because the words had to be easy to understand, there was usually only one melodic line at a time, based on a simple orchestral accompaniment.

With the development of vocal and instrumental music, the modes were replaced by new melodic patterns, which we recognize as those of the major and minor scales. The strong rhythms of songs and dances lent vitality to the beat. Composers learned how to support a melody with rich harmonic accompaniments, without drowning it in a sea of sound. To help them along, vocal techniques were developing as more demands were made upon the singers, and some of the powerful new voices would have been difficult for even a brass band to drown out.

The stage on which operas were given was also transformed, with an effect that was long-lasting. The stage of Shakespeare's day was an apron, which projected into the audience. The *commedia dell' arte* troupes performed on open-air platforms which were also surrounded by their audiences. Neither type of stage was suitable to opera. For that matter, neither were the drawing rooms in the palaces of the nobility, where the first works were given by small casts for small audiences with small orchestras.

As opera became a public form of entertainment, it first took over theatres that had been built for other purposes. But soon new theatres were constructed chiefly for operatic performances. In these new opera houses, the *proscenium* stage became standard, all the action taking place within a framework that separated actors from audience. The proscenium stage had its advantages for many spoken dramas as well, but for such plays as those of Shakespeare it was less suitable than the apron stage, and some modern directors and critics still resent the fact that opera drove platform and apron stages out of the theatre.

The proscenium stages were fully equipped with trap doors and mechanical devices, so that they could handle the huge casts, the changes of scene, and the spectacular stage effects the public was eager to see. In 1680, the most spectacular of spectacles was produced as an opera called *Berenice Vendicativa (Berenice)* by Domenico Freschi, with a cast of four hundred people, two lions, two elephants, several hundred horses, and a stable filled with wild boar, deer, and bears. This crowd of singers and extras, with its more or less trained zoo, would have been impossible to maneuver in the palaces of the Florentine noblemen who patronized the *Camerata*.

The noblemen, however, were not forgotten in the new opera houses. Along with the introduction of the proscenium stage went the development of the audience's half of the house. The common people were allowed in, but only to fill the less important seats. Elaborately decorated boxes were reserved for the rich and noble, while marble sculptures and columns, great mirrors, and the light of thousands of candles added an air of luxury which made them feel at home. Long winding staircases were provided so that the ladies in the audience could sweep down them in elaborate gowns to make an entrance or an exit as fine as any on stage. The tradition of going to the opera to be seen as well as to see and hear developed early.

The evolution of opera, like that of a biological species, took place as a struggle for existence against competing forms of entertainment, some of them much less expensive. The *commedia dell' arte,* for instance, despite a few famous troupes who were exceptions to the general rule, was usually performed with music and plots for which no composer or dramatist received credit or payment, on a platform that cost nothing to put up, by actors who were lucky if they received enough to live on. The opera, on the other hand, had to pay a composer and often a librettist (not always, because at times a composer used a libretto that had been used before). It needed a special theatre, not to speak of elaborate stage equipment, and required the services of expensive singers. It had to charge a relatively high admission fee, and if it hoped to survive at all, could do so only by adapting itself to the needs and desires of its audienes. In the process of adaptation, it borrowed from its rivals. Without apology, it lifted the comic scenes and characters from the *commedia dell' arte,* the stage spectacles from the old mystery plays, songs and choruses from pastorales, and the idea of prologues and overtures from the *intermedios* of serious plays.

We have seen similar battles for survival in our own modern entertainment world. The early movies had to compete against stage plays, and borrowed from the stage not only actors but plots and techniques. Then they developed their own techniques —whereupon the stage promptly stole back what it could. Later, with the growth of radio and television, both new forms of entertainment borrowed from stage and movies, with which they were in deadly competition.

The life-and-death struggle involved in some of these borrowings can be seen most clearly when we consider the attempts to export opera from Italy to other countries. Italian opera had been performed in Germany as early as 1618 and in France not much later. In Germany there was a language difficulty. Not many of the German nobility understood Italian, and opera could not establish itself firmly in Germany until it was written in the language of the country.

In France the chief difficulty was of another nature. The court had gone mad about ballet, and opera had no chance for serious competition until in 1673 the composer Jean Baptiste Lully managed to find a successful formula. Lully was able to blend Italian opera with French tragedy as well as with the old pastorales, and he incorporated ballet scenes into his production. He was so successful that from 1673 to his death in 1687 he had a monopoly in French operatic productions. His operas were rather specially designed, not to amuse the whole of the French court, but only the French king, Louis XIV. As the king considered himself all of France, whatever pleased him was supposed, automatically, to please the nation. Hence, all Lully's operas, the librettos for which were written chiefly by Phillipe Quinault, began with prologues that glorified the king.

Lully was successful not only in flattering his royal master but also in adapting opera to the needs of the French language. In patterning his recitative (music half-spoken, half-sung) after the style of declamation evolved by French tragedians, Lully returned in some respects to the original ideals of the *Camerata,* although by now, of course, the theories of this group had lost most of their direct influence. Lully's operas demanded clearer enunciation of the words, which must not be drowned out by the music and, as an additional aid to understanding, the composer eliminated the dazzling vocal displays that had become customary among Italian singers.

Both opera and ballet flourished in France, the operas of Lully being followed by those of Jean Philippe Rameau. He was a greater composer than Lully, but his work was handicapped by poor librettos. Meanwhile, some of the older forms of entertainment, like the pastorale, the miracle plays, and eventually the *commedia dell' arte,* their useful elements absorbed by more modern forms of theatre, gradually lost their audiences and gave up the ghost.

In England the opera managed to gain a foothold by adapting itself to the popular masque. This was an entertainment in which the plot, involving allegorical or mythical characters, served as an excuse for introducing spectacles, dances, songs, and instrumental selections, all tied together with spoken dialogue. The masque was not yet opera. Its plot was usually even more disjointed than was the plot in Venetian opera, and it lacked musical consistency, its songs being a collection of old arias and new compositions, without musical connecting links between one scene and the next. But it prepared its audiences for opera.

In England opera also had to compete with the plays of Shakespeare and other great dramatists. Following the usual custom of borrowing from their competitors, librettists and composers adapted both *The Tempest* and *Macbeth,* by Shakespeare, to operatic form. They introduced songs, ballets, instrumental selections, and a multitude of spectacular stage effects. *The Tempest* offered an occasion for scenes of shipwreck and magic, *Macbeth* for violent duels and battles. Scenes were altered, language changed, and new characters added at will.

England did have one great composer of opera in Henry Purcell, whose *Dido and Aeneas* is still revived today. Purcell's life was unfortunately short, however, and he had only a brief influence on English music.

Although opera had severe competition elsewhere, it retained its popularity in Italy, and followed the same pattern as in that first opera house in Venice. By the middle of the seventeenth century, the singer was dominant in Italian opera. He was to remain so for more than a century. Sopranos ruled the stage as powerful princes, under a weak king, ruled a country. Most composers could choose the subject, write the music, and make whatever musical and technical innovations they pleased, though occasionally, when a librettist had a considerable reputation, the composer had to use a libretto given to him. If his music furthered the glory of the singer, well and good. If the singer felt that the music slighted his (or her) abilities, he would change it as he pleased, and if the whim seized him, refuse to do an aria at all or tell the composer how he wanted it rewritten. If the composer was unable or unwilling to follow instructions, the singer might bring in his own private composer.

Under such conditions, it is all the more striking that great composers continued to be attracted to opera. The center of Italian opera shifted from Venice to Naples, and "Neapolitan opera" was exported all over Europe. Possibly the greatest of its composers was Alessandro Scarlatti, whose musical career spanned not only the end of the seventeenth century but the first quarter of the eighteenth. Scarlatti wrote more than a hundred operas, and developed the habit of ending the first two acts of his serious operas with comic scenes. Whatever effect this had artistically, it did away with the insertion of a comic intermezzo, or intermediate scene unrelated to the opera, between the acts.

Among the other composers worth noting is Niccolò Porpora, not so much because he had any striking ability for creating great music, but because in one way he characterizes the entire era. Porpora, whose life stretched from 1686 to 1767, was perhaps the greatest singing teacher who ever lived, and with his prejudice in favor of the singer, as against the song, he wrote arias full of dazzling vocal displays. His operas are forgotten. His pupils are remembered as the most famous singers of their age.

A more modest composer, and unfortunately a short-lived one, was Giovanni Pergolesi, whose life lasted only from 1710 to 1736. In 1733, Pergolesi wrote *La Serva Padrona (The Servant as Mistress),* a short opera bouffe, which is fresh and musically interesting, and is produced even now.

A contemporary of Porpora, George Frideric Handel, was a great composer of both vocal and instrumental works. Handel had the double misfortune, for a composer of opera, to be born in Germany and to work in England. During the early years of the eighteenth century, while he was trying to write opera in competition with the imported product, he was still dependent mainly upon Italian singers, but he was less tolerant of their arrogance than the Italian composers, and his threat to drop a soprano out of the window was only one of many displays of temper. It was also annoying that, on the London stage, Italian singers sang Italian while the other singers sang English in the same opera. This may have "improved" the plot by making it incomprehensible, but it also annoyed a good part of the audience.

Handel's operas lacked good librettos, and they are rarely performed today. But his music has not lost its beauty and individual arias are heard frequently on the concert stage.

In his own day, the death-blow to Handel's hopes in opera came not from his Italian rivals, but from a completely unexpected source. The year 1728 saw the production of *The Beggar's Opera,* which was not an opera at all in the strict sense, but a *ballad opera,* for the music was a medley of songs and airs, long familiar to the British public. But this very familiarity made the music popular, and the ironic nature of the story, with an excellent libretto by John Gay, helped make it a tremendous success. Its tale of thieves, beggars, and prostitutes made the stories of gods, goddesses, and heroes seem ridiculous, and drew the audiences away from Italian-style operas. (Two centuries later, adapted for the modern stage by Kurt Weill and Berthold Brecht,

A production of The Beggar's Opera *by John Gay. The drawing has been credited to Hogarth.*

as *The Threepenny Opera,* it was equally successful. It played in an Off Broadway theatre in New York continuously for five years.) Handel stopped writing great music for indifferently successful operas, and wrote great oratorios instead. He had the gloomy satisfaction of seeing his Italian rivals withdraw from London equally defeated.

Only a few years later, in 1735, the first ballad opera was performed in the American colonies. This was a work called *Flora, or Hob in the Well,* put together to a libretto by John Hippisley, and given in Charleston, South Carolina. Not until 1791 did the American continent see, in New Orleans, its first performance of what was supposed to be genuine opera, given by a troupe of French comedians.

Even at the height of the domination of opera by the singers, French opera never forgot the traditions of Lully. Ballet retained its popularity in the operas produced in Paris, and if the composer had to cater to the passion for dance, at least he was less subservient to the singer. But France and England were not alone in their growing resentment of all the follies that resulted from the singer's supremacy. Even in Italy the singers had their enemies, chiefly the librettists and the composers. Arias were the high spots of an opera, and each leading singer had to have one aria in each act. This requirement reduced the entire opera to a series of arias linked by *recitativo secco* —dry declamations, with a sparse accompaniment—which were supposed to carry on the plot, but failed to do so because the audience knew the plot and preferred to carry on its own conversations instead.

Polite auditors stopped talking when the recitative ended and an aria began. But for many individuals the opera was a social occasion, and while waiting for the aria, large numbers of people played cards or chess, ate fruits and pies, and chatted.

At first every attempt to challenge the singers met with failure, but a reaction was bound to set in. The change finally came with Christoph Willibald Gluck, a German, who first had a successful career in Italian opera. By the time he was thirty-one he had composed ten operas that were produced successfully in Milan and elsewhere in Italy. He was not a reformer then, but the seeds of revolt were obviously in him, for Pietro Metastasio, the great writer of librettos of that day, called him a composer of fire, but mad. Metastasio was compared by his contemporaries to Homer and Dante, which gives us some idea of his reputation as a poet. The reputation has not survived, but his judgment of Gluck was perceptive.

Gluck's madness, however, if that is the right word, remained under control until 1750, when he married in Vienna. His wife presented him with a gift that brought out the best in him—a large dowry. Encouraged by his new-found financial independence, Gluck began to strike out for musical independence as well.

In 1755 he was asked to conduct performances of French *opéra comique* (see glossary), altered somewhat to conform to Viennese taste. He composed new airs for these operas, and in doing so, learned to adapt his music more closely to the poetry than he had done for Italian opera. Then he was asked to compose the music to a ballet, *Don Juan,* which would serve to illustrate the principles of the ballet master Jean-Georges Noverre. Noverre's chief principle was that everything should be simple and natural. In a revolt against much that was artificial and affected, the "back-to-nature" movement of that time was becoming very fashionable indeed.

Gluck made this new tendency very explicit when he wrote his new opera, *Orfeo ed Euridice,* first performed in 1762. In his preface to the published edition of a later opera, *Alceste* (1767), Gluck proclaimed his artistic principles. His desire, he said, was "to animate the figures without altering their contours." This was a return to the original desire of the *Camerata,* but not to their methods. Gluck did not minimize but emphasized the importance of the music. It was to be genuine melody, not merely a string of vocal flourishes. He eliminated both the flowery coloratura passages and the dry passages of recitative that customarily linked them, and wrote instead operas filled with continuously dramatic and beautiful music.

The quality of the music was in fact so high that it overcame the weaknesses of the opera as a whole. *Orpheus and Eurydice,* enchanting as it was to the opera audiences of Gluck's day, did not have the impulse of a genuinely dramatic story, which drove

A production by Herbert Graf of Gluck's Iphigenia in Aulis *presented in the Boboli Gardens in Florence, Italy. Outdoor productions of opera are not uncommon in Europe.*

from one event to the next, but was rather a series of loosely connected scenes, Nevertheless, by contrast with the Italian operas of that time, it was a masterpiece of dramatic construction. It retains its interest even today, though it is now performed for the beauty of the music rather than for any dramatic qualities.

Gluck's later operas, including *Alceste, Iphigénie en Aulide* (1774), and *Iphigénie en Tauride* (1779), showed the development of his abilities as a musical dramatist, the last being often considered his masterpiece. But it is *Orpheus and Eurydice* that is most often produced today.

While Gluck was carrying out one revolution in serious opera, another was taking place in comic opera. We have seen how comic scenes, first introduced between the acts of a serious opera, soon crept into the opera itself. By the end of the seventeenth century, comic episodes turned up in the most unlikely places, ruining any hope of a serious dramatic effect.

Pietro Metastasio, if he was not a Homer or a Dante, was still of sufficient poetic stature to help abolish such abuses. He wrote twenty-seven librettos, which became the basis of more than a thousand operas, and he fought against the introduction of irrelevant comic scenes. He was helped in his fight by the growth of *opera buffa* as a separate form. This permitted all the comic scenes to be lumped together and performed without interfering with the serious drama of the evening.

Opera buffa was farcical (or comic) opera, and as the first productions were short, and meant only as relief from serious dramatic fare, they were on trivial or absurd themes. Entrusted to less skilled singers than the serious operas, as well as to inferior actors, they usually parodied the serious operas.

During the eighteenth century, however, the themes changed and, along with them, the nature of the comedy. Middle-class comedy replaced the traditional farcical plots handed down by the *commedia dell' arte*. Burlesque arguments between gods and goddesses gave way to scenes of domestic misunderstanding, of master and servant at cross purposes, or of husband and wife trying to deceive each other. This new comedy was not out of place in serious opera, nor for that matter were serious scenes out of place in full-length comic operas. By the end of the century there was little to distinguish comic from serious opera. All operas were serious enough to have reasonably consistent plots and to deal with genuine characters, while they tried to be comic in words and action, as well as in music.

By this time the possibilities of humor in music were being explored. Sopranos and tenors had always seemed funny to some people, but unintentionally so. Now composers learned to use the bass voice for deliberately comic effects, contrasting its deep rumble with the shrill tones of a soprano. As orchestral technique improved, the extreme sounds of different instruments, from the piping of the piccolo to the growl of the double bass, were used. This carried out the ideas of the long-forgotten *Camerata,* that the music should interpret the feeling of the words. But the feeling now interpreted was comic instead of tragic.

Among the famous operas of the period were *Il Barbiere di Siviglia (The Barber of Seville),* by Giovanni Paisiello, first performed in 1782. This became such a favorite that when Gioacchino Rossini later wrote his own *Il Barbiere de Siviglia* in 1816, audiences resented his impudence. Now of course, it is Rossini's *Barber* that is famous and Paisiello's that is almost forgotten. Domenico Cimarosa's *Il Matrimonio Segreto (The Secret Marriage),* first performed in 1792, was another favorite. The overture is occasionally played nowadays, the opera less often.

The operas of this period that are still played regularly, not for the purpose of reverent revival but for enjoyment, are those of Wolfgang Amadeus Mozart. Mozart was in some ways the most remarkable musician who ever lived. A child prodigy who gave piano recitals from the age of five or six, he differed from the hundreds of other child prodigies in the history of music because his musical powers continued to grow almost to the day he died. He composed vocal and instrumental music of all kinds that was beautiful as pure sound, while at the same time he was unequalled in using music to express the feelings of his operatic characters.

He wrote his first symphony at the age of four, and his first *opera buffa, La Finta Semplice (The Pretended Simpleton),* in Italian, a few years later, in 1768. About the same time, at the age of twelve, he wrote *Bastien und Bastienne,* a *Singspiel* or Songplay, a German form of comic opera. This was performed in the garden of Dr. Anton Mesmer, who had discovered the wonders of hypnotism, and was using his discovery in attempts to cure disease. Two years later Mozart wrote his first serious opera, *Mitridate, rè di Ponto (Mithridates, King of Pontus).*

These works of his childhood are occasionally played now. They have enough musical interest to be heard with enjoyment, as well as amazement. But the works that established Mozart's fame as a composer of opera came later. *The Marriage of Figaro,* performed in Vienna in 1786, was based on a sequel to *The Barber of Seville,* originally a play by Beaumarchais. The libretto, by Lorenzo da Ponte, is an excellent one, but the characters, as they express themselves in words, are only the skeletons of the flesh and blood characters Mozart creates with his music. Then came *Don Giovanni,* produced in Prague in 1787, less comic than *The Marriage of Figaro,* but with characterization just as remarkable and with even more magnificent music.

In 1790, Vienna saw the production of Mozart's *Così fan tutte* (*Thus Do All Women*), an *opera buffa,* and the following year came *La Clemenza di Tito (The Clemency of Titus),* a serious opera that Mozart tossed off in eighteen days while preoccupied with other work, writing symphonies (forty-one of them in his short life), piano concertos, violin concertos, and works for small groups of all kinds, while preparing and giving concerts and trying desperately to make a living.

As an adult Mozart also wrote two *Singspiels* that are still performed—*Die Entführung aus dem Serail* (*The Elopement from the Seraglio*) (1782), and *Die Zauberflöte* (*The Magic Flute*) (1791), the latter being handicapped by an especially confusing and complicated plot. We are not sure who concocted the libretto, although it was probably Emanuel Schikaneder, an actor and manager of a small theatre. It appears that Mozart or Schikaneder became dissatisfied with the story after the music for Act I had already been composed. As the scheduled per-

Left: *Emanuel Schikaneder, librettist of Mozart's* The Magic Flute, *who appeared as Papageno in the first production of the opera. Drawing by Ignaz Alberti.* Below: *A scene from the first performance of* The Magic Flute *in Vienna, 1791.*

The Prison Yard scene from Beethoven's opera, Fidelio, *as performed at the Covent Garden Opera House in England.*

formance was near at hand, only minor alterations could be made in the part already written, while the story was sent off on a new tack.

It is a tribute to Mozart's musical genius that despite this lack of clarity he could make his characters interesting and bring the opera to life. Like other Mozart operas, it is played not out of a spirit of respect for the dead or dying, but because audiences like it.

Another great musician, Ludwig van Beethoven, is known as an operatic composer only for his *Fidelio,* which was a failure when first performed in 1805, but a success in revised form in 1815. Beethoven had difficulty in applying his genius to the operatic form, and is much better known as a composer of symphonies and chamber music.

German opera reached a peak in 1821 with *Der Freischütz* (*The Marksman*), by Carl Maria von Weber. This made use of songs and dances in a story dealing with the struggle of a hero against that ever popular villain, the devil. The fine overture, based upon the melodies of the opera itself, is performed even more frequently than the opera. *Der Freischütz* was so thoroughly German in its music and its approach that it almost put an end for the time to Italian opera in Germany, as a century before *The Beggar's Opera* had put an end to Italian opera in England. Weber's subsequent operas, *Euryanthe* (1823), and *Oberon* (1826), also contain beautiful music, but on the whole are less highly regarded.

Possibly of lesser calibre as a musician, but even more successful in his own sphere, was Gioacchino Rossini. Rossini had a brilliant career in Italy, which included the production of his *Barber of Seville* at Rome in 1816. This youthful masterpiece marks a high point of comic opera. It is not in a class, musically, with the work of Mozart, but for that matter what opera is? Rossini's *Barber* has virtues of its own, precisely the virtues that a comic opera should have: liveliness, gaiety, an unfailing flow of melody that, if not profound, at least always sparkles on the surface, and continual rhythmic excitement. A hundred and fifty years after its first performance, it still keeps an audience interested and laughing.

After a few years of success in Italy, Rossini spent a season in London, and then, in 1824, went to Paris. The center of the opera world had shifted dramatically from the early days of the eighteenth century. With the success of Gluck's works, Paris had become the dominant city of opera. Its rule was not absolute, as was shown by the first production of Mozart's operas in such cities as Vienna and Prague, and of *Der Freischütz* in Berlin. But it was definitely the capital of the reformed art, and it re-

Gioacchino Rossini, composer of The Barber of Seville, William Tell, *and other operas.*

tained this position through the first half of the nineteenth century.

It should be noted that the older form of opera, even after its defeat by Gluck, retained its popularity in Italy. The famous La Scala opera house of Milan, seating 3,600 people, was

Interior of La Scala in Milan as it was in the 1830s.

opened in 1778, and its productions have remained successful for almost two centuries.

However, it was to Paris that Rossini went to test his mettle. Here he caused as much of a sensation as he had in his own country. His career reached its climax in 1829, with the production of *Guillaume Tell* (*William Tell*). And then, at little more than the age at which Mozart had stopped composing, Rossini also stopped composing operas. But it had taken death to end Mozart's career, while Rossini lived on almost forty years longer, rich, respected, and producing only piano and vocal works, and some church pieces. His reasons for deserting opera composition have never been fully understood.

William Tell was one of the new productions that were replacing the comic opera. Known as "grand opera," these works, like the old serious opera, originally had no spoken dialogue. They gave large-scale treatment to serious themes, of which revolt against tyranny was the most popular. Paris, we must remember, was not only the center of opera but the breeding ground of the French Revolution, and revolutions had broken out or were threatening all over Europe. Beethoven's *Fidelio,* like Rossini's *William Tell* deals with revolt against a tyrant. *La Muette de Portici (The Dumb Girl of Portici),* a work by Daniel Auber, a musician much inferior to Rossini, and, of course, to Beethoven, touched off a popular revolution in Brussels in 1830, resulting a year later in the formation of Belgium as a separate state.

The very titles of some of these new operas reveal much about their nature. *Les Huguenots (The Huguenots),* by Giacomo Meyerbeer, is a story of religious persecution. *Les Troyens (The Trojans),* by Hector Berlioz, is the story of an entire people fleeing for safety, and has the scope of an epic. The new "grand" opera was obviously adapted to the tastes of the Parisians in many ways—not only in choice of theme, but also because of the spectacular production. Ballets were obligatory, of course, as were processions and crowd scenes. Orchestras also grew in size. Scores became longer and more complicated, choruses were written for the crowds, solo parts were expanded.

There was no longer any question of indulging the vanity of singers. At this stage of operatic history the composer told the singer what to do, often much to the singer's distress. Sopranos and tenors complained that they had to strain their voices and produce ugly sounds instead of the pretty trills and arpeggios that had so pleased the old audiences. The composers, however, wanted not prettiness but dramatic effect, and dramatic effect they got.

The old distinction between *opéra comique* and serious (or

grand) opera became more and more blurred. Only a technical distinction remained: comic opera included some spoken dialogue —often only a few sentences—while serious opera had none. But this distinction became less meaningful as composers began to create more new forms of opera. Light opera, romantic opera, and operetta came into existence alongside serious opera, comic opera, grand opera, and *opera buffa.*

At this point, many familiar names crowd the history of opera. Jacques Offenbach wrote operettas such as *Orphée aux enfers (Orpheus in Hades)* in 1859, and Johann Strauss, Jr. wrote *Die Fledermaus (The Bat)* in 1874. Neither is a great work, but both are still alive. The absurdity of definitions becomes evident when we consider the story of *Faust,* by Charles Gounod. Staged in 1859 as *opéra comique,* it was soon modified, recitatives being substituted for spoken dialogue. As grand opera, *Faust* became the most popular of all French operas.

Meanwhile, in Italy, a new generation of composers was growing up. Gaetano Donizetti wrote with as much facility as Rossini. Possibly inferior as a musician, he attained success with such works as the opera buffa *L'elisir d'amore (The Elixir of Love)* in 1832, and the serious *Lucia di Lammermoor* in 1835. Both are still performed. Vincenzo Bellini's *Norma,* produced in 1831, became still another favorite. But Donizetti, Bellini, and the other Italian composers soon fell into the shade when a new star—Fortunio Giuseppe Francesco Verdi—was born in 1813. From about 1842, the year that saw the production of his *Nabucco,* almost till the day of his death in 1901, Verdi dominated Italian opera.

Nabucco is an example of the appeal that contributed to Verdi's success. Not one of his better works, it aroused enthusiasm because of its story, which deals with the persecution of the ancient Hebrews at the time of Nabucco, or Nebuchadnezzar. This account of ancient persecution was regarded by Italian audiences as a veiled reference to their own struggle against foreign rule. In the middle of the nineteenth century, Italy was a divided country in the grip of the Austrian monarchy, and its efforts to achieve liberation and unity were symbolized by the figure of one man—the king. Verdi's name represented this symbol: *Vittorio Emmanuel Re d'Italia,* or Victor Emmanuel, King of Italy. When the crowds cheered, "Viva Verdi," they were cheering for their own freedom.

Verdi's career did not depend merely on the possession of a magic name. He was the possessor of a tremendous musical genius, which, toward the end of his life, was most fully expressed. His works include such familiar operas as *Un ballo in Maschera (A Masked Ball), Il Trovatore (The Troubadour), La Traviata (The Erring Woman), Rigoletto, La Forza del Destino (The Power of Destiny),* and *Macbeth.* In 1871, when he was fifty-eight, *Aïda* was produced. By 1874, however, when he wrote his *Requiem,* a religious composition that sounds like an opera, he felt that his days as a composer were finished.

But it turned out that his greatest triumphs lay ahead. In 1887 he produced his tragic *Otello,* the music of which rises to heights he never before attained. More subtle, less immediately successful than such works as *Aïda, Otello* has been growing in popular and critical esteem for three quarters of a century. Verdi's *Falstaff,* of 1893, the year he was eighty, is a masterpiece of *opera buffa.*

To go back slightly, the year of 1842, in which Verdi's *Nabucco* was produced, was also the year of the production, in Dresden, Germany, of *Rienzi,* by Richard Wagner. *Rienzi,* based on a novel by Bulwer-Lytton, was a grand opera with a theme (taken from history) of revolt against tyranny. An immediate success, the recognition it brought Wagner made possible the production of his *Der Fliegende Holländer (The Flying Dutchman)* in 1843 and *Tannhaüser* in 1845. These were less successful than *Rienzi,* but are more often performed now because modern audiences find them more interesting.

Both operas, but especially *Tannhaüser,* show Wagner's style developing toward the direction he was later to follow. Wagner was getting away from the alternation of set arias and musically unimportant recitative. His melodies were closely adapted to the text, while musical phrases in the orchestra appeared to comment on the words. Wagner called this style *"Sprechgesang,"* ("Speech Song"). It had been used before him by others, especially by Weber, who was in many ways his model. But Wagner used it to a greater extent than any one else and showed its possibilities. This wasn't easy, for *Sprechgesang* puzzled the singers, who considered it highly unmusical, and most of them sang it unmusically to prove their point.

Wagner, however, was relying less and less on the singers and more on the orchestra. He had a vision of opera as a form of dramatic art in which poetry, music, dance, architecture, and painting all contributed to the dramatic expression. The singers, the orchestra, the stage setting, and the opera theatre itself were to be only means to that great end.

Wagner had contempt for what was called "grand opera," and insisted that he did not write any. He wrote "music dramas," and because of his concept of opera as a unified art, he created his own librettos. When he had the chance, he also planned and supervised the building of his own theatre at Bayreuth, Germany.

In his later works, Wagner departed more and more from the general operatic styles of his day. Instead of arias or recitatives in the traditional manner, he created a continuous flow of sound,

Richard Wagner

much of it consisting of *leitmotifs (leading motives)*. These motives were melodic, harmonic, or rhythmic phrases or sentences, sometimes long, sometimes very short. They represented the characters, the actions, and the moods of the drama. By weaving them in and out of the musical pattern, Wagner was able not only to express the action of each scene in the music, but to suggest psychological undertones involving memories of the past and forebodings of the future. Critics agree on the identity of some *leitmotifs* but not all, and they therefore give different estimates of the number in any single music drama.

Wagner was able to compose as he did, not because of his theories but because of the whole bent of his musical thought. He gradually developed a technique of composition suited to his ideas, and when he actually sat down to compose, as he himself confessed, he forgot his theories.

Among his famous works are *Lohengrin, Tristan und Isolde, Die Meistersinger von Nürnberg (The Mastersingers of Nürnberg), Parsifal,* and the cycle of *Der Ring des Nibelungen (The Ring of the Nibelung)*, which consists of four music dramas: *Das Rheingold (The Rhine Gold), Die Walküre (The Valkyries), Siegfried,* and *Die Götterdämmerung (Twilight of the Gods)*. The Ring cycle is based on mythological subjects and is laden with symbolism. As usual with such works, critics disagree as to their inner meaning, and Wagner's own interpretation of the symbols is not very convincing.

It is part of the irony of operatic history that despite Wagner's contempt for "grand opera," his own music dramas are referred to as operas, and despite his insistence that poetry, music, and all the arts formed one unified whole, it is the music that has kept his works alive. Orchestral preludes and vocal selections from Wagner's music dramas appear frequently on concert programs and hold their own, without the aid of scenery, dance, or the audience's knowledge of the plot, but his librettos, like most librettos, cannot stand on their own feet either as poetry or drama without support from the music.

Wagner had a tremendous influence on other composers. It became fashionable for a time, even in French and Italian opera, to use *leitmotifs* to identify characters and situations. But the method could not be used to the extent that Wagner used it, for several reasons. First, it required habits of musical thought that few composers were able to acquire. It demanded tremendous technical ability to use the same group of *leitmotifs* in completely different situations to express different moods. And, finally, composers realized that other ways of expression were possible, often more in harmony with their own manner of thought.

Even during the Wagnerian heyday, most French and Italian opera continued in essentially traditional courses. Georges Bizet's *Carmen,* produced in 1875, is a masterpiece that owes little if anything to Wagner. *Lakmé* (1883), by Léo Delibes, *Samson et Dalila* (1877) by Camille Saint-Saëns and *Thaïs* (1894), by Jules Massenet are popular works of that period that are still occasionally played. Though they were not operas of the first rank, they were composed and successfully performed without making concessions to Wagner's ideas. Gustave Charpentier's *Louise* is another popular French opera, produced in 1900, which, in its realism, was far removed from the grandiose symbolism of Wagner.

Symbolism of a different kind is represented by Claude Debussy's *Pelléas et Mélisande,* first performed in 1902. Where Wagner had demanded a massive orchestra, that could be met on terms of equality only by sopranos and tenors with powerful lungs, Debussy orchestrated quietly and subtly, creating his own melodic patterns and new harmonic and orchestral effects. *Pelléas et Mélisande* is a love story much like Wagner's *Tristan und*

Modest Moussorgsky, composer of Boris Godunov.

Isolde, but where Tristan and Isolde are two definitely flesh and blood people, Pelléas and Mélisande are rather shadowy figures whose very existence appears to be symbolic.

During the nineteenth century, opera developed in Russia. Michael Glinka's *A Life for the Czar,* first performed in 1836, is still performed there under the title *Ivan Susanin.* Peter Ilyich Tchaikovsky wrote two operas still popular in the Soviet Union, *Eugene Onegin* and *Pique Dame (The Queen of Spades).* Both are performed infrequently elsewhere, as is *Prince Igor,* by Alexander Borodin. *Sadko* and *Le Coq d'or (The Golden Cockerel),* both by Nikolai Rimsky-Korsakov, are sometimes given, but the greatest and most powerful of Russian operas is *Boris Godunov,* by Modest Moussorgsky. This still holds the stage all over the world. The libretto, by Moussorgsky himself, was taken from a poem by Alexander Pushkin, the famous Russian poet. Moussorgsky first composed the music in 1868 and 1869, and revised it in 1871 and 1872. It was further revised by Rimsky-Korsakov and other composers in later years, and is an exciting experience in any version.

Native opera was developing in many countries, but perhaps the only operatic composer from a small European country whose work attained world stature is the Czech Bedřich Smetana, composer of much fine music and in particular of *The Bartered Bride,* a comic opera first performed in 1866. The music, although almost all either original with Smetana or completely transformed by him, is based on folk melodies skillfully and beautifully handled.

Italian opera continued to maintain a leading place. Familiar as composers of single well-known operas are the names of Pietro Mascagni for his *Cavalleria Rusticana (Rustic Chivalry)* and Ruggiero Leoncavallo for *I Pagliacci (The Clowns)*. These short

A scene from The Bartered Bride *by Bedřich Smetana, as performed in Brno, Czechoslovakia. This charming opera has also been performed occasionally in English in the United States.*

operas are frequently paired on a double bill. A much more solid reputation is that of Giacomo Puccini, whose *Manon Lescaut, La Bohème, Tosca,* and *Madama Butterfly* enjoy wide popularity and are frequently found on today's programs.

In Germany, Engelbert Humperdinck became known for one opera, *Hänsel und Gretel,* written for children and first performed in 1893. Richard Strauss, on the other hand, wrote for a decidedly adult audience. His *Der Rosenkavalier (The Knight of the Rose), Salome, Electra,* and *Ariadne auf Naxos* have sophisticated themes and sophisticated music as well. All but *Salome* have librettos by Hugo von Hofmannsthal. Strauss used Wagnerian methods but created operas with the stamp of his own individuality. The harmonies are full and the orchestration rich and sensuous.

In strong contrast to the lushness of Strauss is the harsh dissonant music that Alban Berg used in his *Wozzek,* first produced in 1925. So far, *Wozzek* appears to lack popular appeal, but it has impressed critics and artists sufficiently to earn occasional revivals. Dmitri Shostakovich's *Lady Macbeth of Mtsensk,* produced in the Soviet Union in 1934 and later in New York, is another dissonant, violent work. First welcomed, then rejected, in Moscow, it has not been revived.

Opera in the United States has had a relatively short history. The new nation was a mere ten years old when Mozart's *Marriage of Figaro* was produced, and the young country had no orchestra capable of playing Mozart's music, or singers able to sing the vocal parts. It was easier to produce ballad operas imported from England. These were in fact closer to the demands of popular taste. As time went on, however, orchestras developed, and so did audiences. Performances of the great operatic works were given, and American musicians acquired the technique of composition.

Of all American operas, the first to attain genuine popularity was *Porgy and Bess,* written by George Gershwin in a jazz idiom, and first produced in 1935. It has received peculiar treatment at the hands of critics, being rather condescendingly praised for its music, and in some cases damned with the judgment, "Of course, it isn't genuine opera." We have seen that opera includes a tremendous variety of forms, and it is difficult to single out any form as "genuine" at the expense of the others. *Porgy and Bess* has been popular in the United States, and on a world tour it has been accepted as genuinely moving and entertaining.

Also extremely popular is Jerome Kern's *Showboat,* sometimes called a folk opera these days, although it was regarded as simply a musical comedy when first produced in 1927. Actually neither the music nor the story has a folk nature. American operas that have won critical respect, if not popular acclaim include *The King's Henchman* (1927), by Deems Taylor, *Merry Mount* (1934), by Howard Hanson, *Four Saints in Three Acts* (1934), by Virgil Thomson, and *The Emperor Jones* (1933), by Louis Gruenberg. A performance of any of these is a rare event. *Amelia Goes to the Ball* (1937), and *The Medium* (1946), both by Gian-Carlo Menotti have attained greater popularity.

At present, a number of new American operas are being produced with less ambitious objectives and possibly better hope of success. Intended for performance by small companies that can afford no more than modest orchestras or possibly only a piano accompaniment, a few such operas have been well received. But of these, we shall have more to say later.

Meanwhile, there are a few conclusions we can reach from our brief survey of operatic history. First, an opera may be a work in any of a number of extremely different styles, and may appeal to the most varied tastes. It may be serious, comic, or both. It may be long or short, containing the simplest or the most complicated music; it may make the best of sense or be utter nonsense.

If an opera appeals to very few in the composer's own time, it usually dies a quick death. Operatic literature is full of excellent works which had the misfortune to be badly received at their first performances, and never recovered. Only a few, such as Bizet's *Carmen,* were able to overcome a slow start to achieve popularity.

More puzzling is the case of an opera successful in the composer's own day, followed by steady loss of popularity, and eventual disappearance from the repertory. Why should one opera die, while another, judged no better or worse at first performance, continues to live?

Most important to the life or death of an opera is the music. But sometimes, even when the music is great, as in many works of Handel, the opera may still die, and when it is second-rate, as in much of Donizetti, the opera may live.

National taste, helped along by national pride, differs from one country to another, and often keeps operas alive in one small area long after they have been forgotten elsewhere. Italian opera houses schedule performances of Italian operas almost never performed in other countries; Parisians hear French operas that New York never sees or hears; in Moscow and Leningrad, works are given by composers whose very names are unfamiliar to the average American or English opera-goer. Occasionally such national feeling leads to overestimation of local composers. But in helping to keep much beautiful music alive in a period when musical tastes are changing all over the world, and in encouraging the composers of a new generation, it has enormous value, and it is a feeling that Americans should cultivate, provided, of course, the opera is worth keeping alive.

the librettist 2

The early days of opera were golden days for the librettist. His poetry was the opera's excuse for being, and the music was supposed merely to serve his purpose. He could write as he pleased and choose whatever subject appealed to him and his audiences—usually a legend out of some Greek poet or a tale from ancient history. The composer and the singers were called upon merely to intensify the effect of his poetry. And usually it was bad poetry.

From the moment that great composers began to write for opera the situation changed, and the librettist slowly fell back into second place. Then the audiences began to idolize the singers, and things became even worse. Words that were stretched over half a dozen measures, trilled, and adorned with numerous grace notes stopped being words and became mere sounds. They lost their meaning and their importance. The librettist was now asked merely to give the singer an opportunity to perform a solo and not to interfere too much with the music. The composer would seize one or two lines of the poet's text and convert them into the words of an aria, while the narrative portions were lowered to the level of recitative and were disregarded by the audience.

As spectacular stage effects were added to opera, new and easily satisfied demands were made upon the librettist. He was asked to provide an excuse for dancing and for the introduction of battles, processions, miracles, and anything else that would evoke gasps of admiration. The story need not make much sense and frequently it made none at all.

Perhaps this is one reason librettists and composers didn't bother with new stories and told so many of the old ones over and over again. Orpheus was the subject of more than seven hundred operas, as was Iphigenia. Hercules, Jason, and other heroes of Greek mythology appeared time and again.

The reforms of Gluck changed the position of the librettist again, this time slightly for the better. No longer need he be a slave to the singer and the manager of the production. Now he had to serve the composer and has been doing so ever since. For although the libretto is written first, the music of an opera is first in importance. The librettist is asked not merely to compromise on disputed points, as the writer of a spoken play must do when his work is produced, but often to surrender completely whenever there is any sharp conflict with the composer. It is a rare librettist who wins victories over the man who sets his words to music.

Knowledge of this situation colors the librettist's attitude toward his work. His servitude is made tolerable, however, by one fact: if his work is not well done, if the composer counts too greatly on his obedience instead of on his intelligence and literary skill, the libretto will suffer, and so will the opera as a whole. For the composer's own sake, the librettist must be treated as a reasonably well-trusted subordinate, if not as an equal.

The requirements of a libretto differ considerably from those of a spoken play. In the latter, scenes must be carefully prepared in words and action, the characters must be made real, people must behave plausibly, and their behavior must depend on the situation. The action of the play develops from scene to scene. In a libretto, the relation from scene to scene may not be at all obvious. Characters are not developed to the same degree. The librettist may have studied them very thoroughly, but the limitations of space permit him to sketch them only briefly. Changes in behavior seem abrupt and badly motivated—and they would be if the libretto were played without music.

It is the music that makes all the difference. If the librettist were to paint his characters completely there would be no need for the composer. In an opera it is the latter who creates the emotion and who does most of the characterization. It is chiefly the music, and to only a secondary extent the words, that makes the audience accept the reality of a love scene or a death scene. In a play, Tristan and Isolde could express their love for each other for possibly two minutes and exhaust the patience of the audience. In the opera, the music of their love duet stretches on and on, and seems short enough, because it is great music. For the same reason, the audience is willing to let Tristan spend a half hour dying, provided he sings well in his death agony. Are such scenes absurd? Only if we judge by the standards of spoken plays, which do not apply at all.

In opera, transitions take place not only in words but in music. And as emotional scenes are expanded by the needs of the music, the scenes which in spoken drama carry on the story as such are correspondingly compressed, often to little more than a synopsis. Using recitative, one or two of the characters may make clear to the audience what has happened. Then we are in the next emotional or dramatic scene, and the music takes over again.

The librettist must for this reason work closely with the composer. The latter will often choose the characters for whom he wants to write singing parts; he will tell the librettist the mood

Francesco Maria Piave, the librettist of La Traviata, Rigoletto, *and several other operas by Verdi.*

of a scene for which he wants to do the music; he will often decide whether the libretto is to be prose or verse. Sometimes he will choose the rhythm of the verse and even order the librettist to rhyme or not to rhyme, as he thinks the situation demands.

A composer may have such definite ideas about the kind of libretto he wants that no one can satisfy his demands. He may then have to turn librettist himself. Verdi collaborated on the preparation of the libretto of *Aida,* and Wagner wrote all of his, but most composers prefer to divide the labor. Verdi, for one, knew very definitely the kind of libretto he wanted and was able to get it from his collaborators. He insisted on extreme compression, violent shifts in mood, and a tragic plot. Not all composers need the same kind of libretto, but Verdi's requirements were sensible for his type of genius.

A composer may find a libretto unsatisfactory for a number of reasons. Some of the big scenes that the librettist has sketched out may not appeal to him. Perhaps he would rather compress them into a line or two of recitative or dialogue to tell what happened. On the other hand, in the scenes the librettist has slighted, he may see great opportunities, and here he may demand that the librettist use his imagination and expand them. The composer, always aware of the need to end his acts with music that rises to a climax, may find a good opportunity for his skill in a scene the librettist has created—but has placed in the middle of the act. He tells the librettist that he wants the scene put at the end, and now the librettist must rack his brains to fit the change into the plot. Part of Act I may be shifted to Act II; an effective scene that occurs in Act III but is actually superfluous from the point of view of plot development may be shifted to Act I, and so on.

A libretto, like a spoken play, is thus not written but "carpentered," pieces being shifted around to see where they look and sound best, and the edges trimmed until a reasonable fit is secured.

A good example of what a librettist has to do is afforded by Verdi's *Otello,* libretto by Arrigo Boïto. The opera is based on Shakespeare's *Othello,* a play that was written about the time opera was born and had been famous for almost three centuries by the time Verdi came along. The librettist who adapts a very famous play, like the composer who writes the music to it, is in a difficult position. He must not only preserve the poetry of the original and make its plot no less sensible, but must also heighten the emotional effect, or critics and audiences will quite justly demand to know why on earth he bothered to write an opera when the play without music was already so satisfactory.

Shakespeare's *Othello* is in five acts. It has thirteen main characters, plus a host of subsidiary characters such as sailors and messengers. It tells the story of the Moor, Othello, whose love for Desdemona was poisoned with jealousy by the wiles of the villainous Iago. The first act takes place in Venice, and in

Verdi with Boïto, the librettist of Otello *and* Falstaff. *Boïto was also a fine musician and composed the opera,* Méphistophélès.

the first scene we see Iago with Roderigo, a young Venetian who also loves Desdemona. Iago tells why he hates Othello and plans to harm him. The two men arouse Brabantio, Desdemona's father, and set him against Othello. Brabantio complains to the Duke of Venice that Othello has won Desdemona's love by enchantment, but Othello denies this, saying that Desdemona fell in love with him when she heard of the dangers he had lived through, and Desdemona herself confirms his story. The Duke believes Othello, and places him in charge of the Venetian fleet to fight the Turks, who are approaching the island of Cyprus. As the act ends, Iago tells of his plan to inflame Othello's mind with jealousy.

Contrast this with what happens in Boïto's libretto. *Otello* is in four acts instead of five, and there are only nine leading characters—that is, characters who have important singing roles. The Duke of Venice does not appear, nor does Desdemona's father. Act I opens not in Venice but in Cyprus, during a hurricane, accompanied by the thunder and lightning beloved of operatic composers. The people on shore are watching the approach of a Venetian ship which is in danger of being sunk by wind and waves. It is the ship bearing Othello, although at first we do no know this. Iago and Roderigo appear briefly, but as yet we know nothing of their relation to Othello. Then the thunder and lightning subside and Othello appears, safe and sound. He announces that he has fought the Turkish fleet, and that his partial victory has been completed by the storm, which has sunk those ships which survived his onslaught. For several minutes the chorus hails his triumph, and then Iago and Roderigo proceed to tell the audience something of the plot, essentially as it is done in the opening scene of Shakespeare's play. For the first time, *after* the hurricane and the chorus of triumph, we learn what the play is about.

The first act of the opera continues with material from the second act of Shakespeare's play. A huge bonfire is built (this is only talked about in the play) and the chorus hails the flames. This permits a transition to a scene of revelry, in which Iago and Roderigo manage to get Othello's lieutenant, Cassio, drunk. Cassio gets into a brawl and is dismissed from his position by Othello. Desdemona has been aroused by the noise and now arrives, to remain with Othello after every one else has gone. The two sing a duet telling of their love for each other, and the act ends.

The scenes in Venice, which are omitted from the libretto, are not really missed. In Act I, Shakespeare has Othello give reasons for Desdemona's having fallen in love with him. The opera gives the same reasons, but in different form. It begins by *showing* Othello in danger, instead of merely telling about it, and at the end emphasizes why Othello and Desdemona fell in love by having the two speak directly to each other, instead of explaining to the Duke of Venice. The emotional impact, aided by the music, is much greater in the opera.

Although Verdi's Otello *is the most popular of the operas based on the Shakespearean tragedy, he was not the only composer fascinated by the play. Here is a scene from Rossini's* Otello.

In the play, the audience knows the theme of the story from the very first scene. In the libretto, the opening scene, that of the hurricane, is played for its effect as spectacle, and explanations must wait. In the libretto, too, there are scenes, such as that of the chorus hailing the fire, which have little to do with the play. The chorus was introduced for the purpose of making a transition to the scene of revelry, and was apparently expanded for effect.

Is the libretto inferior to the play? Certainly the libretto cannot stand alone, but it was not intended to. Thanks to the music, the love duet of Othello and Desdemona that ends the first act makes the tragedy that will occur all the more poignant, and the libretto is in this respect superior to the play. But the most important lines in this duet are Shakespeare's, and Boïto's achievement was fitting them skillfully into place to suit the needs of an opera. It is the librettist's judgment as to what should be fitted that helps determine the praise or blame he deserves, and here Boïto rates very high.

Whether the librettist adapts a story from a play, a novel, or a myth or starts with an original story of his own, he faces similar problems, not only in plot requirements but in terms of literary quality as well. He must be a poet and have a feeling for the meaning of words, as well as for their sounds and emotional echoes. He need not be a Shakespeare, but he must have at least a little of Shakespeare's technical mastery of words.

It is customary for singers to regard Italian as the ideal language for opera because the vowel endings in Italian words make it the easiest to sing. Try to hold a *t* and you achieve a stutter, an *s*, and all you get is a hiss. English lacks the vowel richness of Italian, but it is not poor in great poetry, nor is German. Russian has combinations of consonants that English-speaking people have difficulty in pronouncing, and French is full of nasal sounds. It is not the language that determines whether or not a libretto is beautiful, but the librettist.

The librettist should therefore know how composer and singer feel about certain sounds, but he must also realize that along with valid rules learned from experience, the traditions of opera include a number of myths that he must disregard. The words, "Speak gently," are rich in consonants, but that does not mean that they cannot be sung beautifully. The use of a high proportion of vowel sounds may make for easier singing, but vowels sung at different pitches are difficult to tell apart, and it is the consonants that permit the listener to understand what is being sung. Intelligibility may seem unimportant to a singer, but the librettist likes his words to be understood, and therefore has a liking for consonants.

He should, of course, introduce those that intensify the emotional effect he and the composer intend to create. The *l* sound, as in *love,* is soft and liquid, the *k* and *g* sounds hard, the *kr* combination, as in crafty, even harder. *Crag* gives an effect of solidity. The feeling aroused by a word or sentence as a whole may overcome the effect of a single consonant, so that the word *kind* does not produce a hard effect, despite the *k* sound. On the whole, however, the librettist must be very conscious of the sounds of his words and must avoid those which counteract the emotional effect of the music, except for purposes of deliberate contrast. He may wish to produce a comic effect, or an effect of insincerity on the part of his character by using soft sounds to a harsh vigorous melody, or vice versa.

For all his skill, the librettist has rarely been well paid. In the early days of opera, a small fee equivalent to possibly twenty-five or fifty dollars was all he could expect. In the eighteenth century, however, the librettist was not without the honor that made up for money, as we have seen in the case of Metastasio, who was ranked with Homer. Gluck's librettist, Calzabigi, had a share in the musical reformation for which Gluck is credited.

In the following century, Eugène Scribe, a fabulously successful playwright, added greatly to his income by writing the librettos of more than a hundred operas. Nowadays, although the librettist can count on royalties instead of a flat fee, he ordinarily expects little. Performances of an opera are usually few compared to those of a play, and in the latter type of work the playwright is usually sole author, while in opera the librettist is the lesser of two collaborators. He receives a small fraction of the successful playwright's income, and only when an opera is sensationally successful, given year after year all over the world, does he receive a worthwhile financial reward for his efforts.

the translator 3

If the original librettist of an opera has a difficult job to do, the translator has an almost impossible one, and is even more poorly rewarded, both financially and in terms of recognition as an artist. He runs into violent opposition at the very beginning, for some people think that opera should not be translated at all. They make a valid point when they insist that in a great opera words and music are so perfectly matched that neither can be changed without losing some of the effect. This is perfectly true. Every time opera is translated, something is lost.

Unfortunately, even more is lost if listeners do not understand the language in which an opera is sung—and most opera-goers in the United States do not understand Italian, French, German, or Russian. Thus the choice becomes one of two evils, and many listeners prefer the evil of translation to the evil of not understanding what they are listening to. Perhaps they recall that an opera is meant to be a drama told in music. Sometimes opera-goers are forced to suffer both evils at once, as when Americans have listened to *Boris Godunov* sung in Italian, a language which divorced the words and music of the Russian original and still left it meaningless to them. Metropolitan Opera patrons also had the honor of hearing their first performance of *Aïda* in completely unsuitable and incomprehensible German.

Granted that translations are worth doing, what makes them practically impossible? The fundamental difficulty is that the translator, unlike the original librettist, is faced with music already written, and this serves as a straitjacket into which the words must be forced. He may have to translate a vowel-rich libretto from the Italian or a consonant-rich one from Russian into English. In the process, he runs across a whole series of problems that it is impossible to solve completely. He is fortunate if he can even approach their solution in a way that will satisfy opera audiences.

Let us illustrate with a very simple example from Richard Strauss's *Der Rosenkavalier.* In the first act, Octavian sings, *"Hier bin ich der Herr,"* or word for word, "Here am I the Master." What is good German is clumsy English. Moreover, the five syllables of German turn into six syllables in English. We can save a syllable by replacing *Master* with *Lord,* but *Lord* would bring up associations of the wrong kind. It is preferable to leave out the word *the* and rearrange the sentence, as the translator has done, to give, "I am Master here." We now have five syllables of good idiomatic English that fit the music well—but not perfectly. In the original, the word *ich, I,* is the third syllable and the most emphatic word of the musical phrase. In the translation, the syllable *Mas* comes third and is emphasized instead. Moreover, the German *ich bin,* with its consonants, has been replaced by *I am,* with its single consonant. There has been an unavoidable change in the effect produced.

A bit further on the German original reads, *"Ich hab ein Glück,"* literally, "I have a good luck" or "happiness." This is not English at all. One desperate translator makes it, "Blest is my lot." The rhythm and the number of syllables have been preserved, along with the idea. But the words have not been translated. A better translation puts it, "I am in luck," which is excellent colloquial English, although here too the meaning has been slightly altered.

The same problems on a vastly larger scale are faced with every libretto that undergoes translation. If the translator has no artistic conscience, the result is sheer absurdity. Two centuries ago, the English writer, Joseph Addison, commented on the idiotic translations of Italian opera that were being inflicted on the London public. Either unimportant words like *the* received great emphasis, being held measure after measure, or the wrong syllable was stressed, or the words were matched with sublime indifference to exactly the wrong music. If a phrase contained the words *high* and *low,* for example, the composer would let the melody rise on *high* and fall on *low*. But a clumsy translator might arrange just the opposite, producing an unintentionally comic effect in what was supposed to be a tragic passage.

Faced with such problems, the translators of librettos translate word for word where they can without sacrifice of literary quality, and paraphrase where such translation would lead to clumsy or impossible English; that is, they give only the general meaning of the foreign words. They rearrange entire sentences, eliminate phrases, introduce new figures of speech where the original figures are too foreign, and in general try to make the libretto sound as if it were written in English in the first place.

To do even a mediocre translation, the translator must know not only the languages from and to which he is translating, but music as well. In this respect he must go far beyond the original librettist, who usually needs to know only one language and, most of the time, need not bother his head about the music at all.

The translator faces even harsher critics than the original librettist. If he paraphrases, he may satisfy the audiences whose native tongue is English, especially if they do not know the language of the original libretto. But a paraphrase is always disconcerting to those who do know the original and find unwelcome novelties in the English version.

It can be seen that translators always manage to displease at least two of the following groups: those who do not like translations at all; those who dislike *literal* translations because they make for stilted English; and those who dislike paraphrases, because a paraphrase is like a new and usually inferior libretto written to the same music. An especially unfortunate translator, of course, displeases everybody. In the past, at least, many translators of opera have been unfortunate. At present opera-goers seem to have had a change of luck, and several excellent translations are available. May their number grow!

the composer 4

To WRITE OPERA successfully, a composer must have a special kind of musical ability. His music must have a dramatic quality. He must be able to translate action and emotion into musical terms, and nowadays he is expected to delineate character in music. It is difficult to generalize further, for some of the most successful composers of pure music have been only moderately successful in opera, or complete failures. The only sure way for a composer to learn whether he is suited for opera or not is to try writing it.

A few operatic composers, like Mozart and Richard Strauss, have been equally famous for their non-operatic works as well. Most composers of opera, however, owe their fame almost exclusively to opera itself, although many of them have composed other music which is little known to the general public.

The composer of opera must write music that singers will be able to sing, and want to sing. When we consider the endless quarrels between singers and composers that have taken place ever since opera was born, we wonder whether the composer ever pleased the singers, or vice versa. Sometimes it seems to a composer that a singer exists only to mangle his beautiful music, and to the singer that a composer's whole mission in life is to frustrate him by not permitting him to display his voice. These emotional reactions, however, need not obscure the fact that singers and composers need each other. Their quarrels are family quarrels, and always end in reconciliation. Unless they do, there is no opera.

Assuming that he has the right sort of talent or genius, how does the composer set about writing an opera? In the first place, what opera shall he write? In the seventeenth century—as in Venice, with its numerous opera houses—and even a century later, it was easy to find the answers to these questions. Opera was so popular, and so definitely restricted in type of plot, that a composer could take not only the same story but the very same libretto that had served a previous composer, and write new music to it. Hence the endless Orpheuses and Iphigenias, the countless repetitions of the story of Hercules, of Theseus and Ariadne, and of Admetus.

Eventually these stories would be done to death, but even so, after a suitable interval, they could be resurrected for new audiences. There was wisdom in choosing them, for it can be assumed that myths which have survived for two thousand years have qualities that make for popularity. And indeed these stories had those very elements of love and tragic conflict that we think of as synonymous with the operatic art.

As time went on, however, this happy situation changed. Audiences became less aristocratic and more middle class, and they began to want stories that were related to their own lives and interests. Myths and classical subjects, of course, never went completely out of fashion, but the method of treatment changed. No longer could the story be told "straight." It had to be treated ironically and lightly, as Offenbach did in *Orpheus in Hades,* or be laden with psychological symbolism, as in Stravinsky's opera-oratorio *Oedipus Rex.*

Composers began to pay much more attention to their librettos, as they do today. The great geniuses of music could no longer be confident that their powers would transform even the most commonplace plot and dialogue into a work of art. A great symphonic master like Beethoven was so unsure of himself when it came to opera that he spent months and years in a search for the right subject, and underwent mental tortures over the libretto. In the end, he wrote only one opera, *Fidelio,* and that has never been more than moderately successful.

Personal preference became important, as well as the ability to judge literary works. It was necessary for the subject to come to life for the individual composer. Debussy was an extremely skillful musician, but it is difficult to imagine him writing an opera to the libretto of *Fidelio,* or of *The Marriage of Figaro,* with its down-to-earth characters, just as it is difficult to imagine Mozart or Beethoven writing an opera to the libretto of *Pelléas and Mélisande.*

That is one reason for the numerous consultations with the librettist. The different scenes must invoke in the composer emotional, dramatic, or comic feelings that he can translate into his kind of music. He will insist that every scene be shaped to his personal requirements.

Another reason concerns the direct musical implications of the libretto. To the librettist the characters he creates are people. To the composer they are also soprano, tenor, bass, and so on, and he must make sure that the action brings them together in the right duets, trios, or other groups for the kind of singing he has in mind. He must decide what is to be sung and what is to be spoken or done as recitative. Here there must be give and take between him and the librettist, who will bow to the composer's will at most points, but will often draw the line at distorting his characters for the sake of an effective aria or duet.

Ludwig van Beethoven, whose only opera, Fidelio, *dealt with the heroic theme of liberation from tyranny.*

This problem too was much simpler to solve in the days when the singers ruled opera. Then there were customarily six leading singers, and each had at least one aria in each set. Every librettist and composer knew the requirements, and met them automatically, both audience and singers being happy with the result, whether or not the aria at any particular point made dramatic sense. The recitatives were regarded merely as so many links between arias, and as it was customary to pay no attention to recitative, the opera as a whole became almost a series of vocal solos.

For about one hundred and fifty years, however, this early formula of an aria for each singer in each act has been more and more disregarded, and the composer must devise his own effective musical arrangement. This, of course, depends on the libretto, and may take many months to work out to his satisfaction.

When it comes to the actual business of musical composition, the result depends on the composer's own genius, which is another name for musical imagination, and on the techniques of musical composition he has acquired. Technique comes from study, training, and continual practice in composing and staging operas so that the composer learns from his own experience and can correct mistakes in succeeding works.

Technique is extremely important when a composer lacks it, but in itself it does not make for great or even passable music, as has been discovered by hundreds of well-trained musicians who have composed thousands of forgotten operas. On its lowest level, technique requires a moderate amount of intelligence, but no actual musical talent. For instance, the rules of counterpoint, which is the art of writing one melody against another, are less complicated than the rules of high school algebra, and can be mastered even by a man who is tone deaf. They have, in fact, been "learned" by machines, which can write what is called "music." But the productions of machines or of tone-deaf composers are not yet able to compete with the compositions of Gluck or Verdi.

Another example of the usefulness as well as the limitations of technique is this: it is part of the composer's training to learn to write arias, or solos for leading characters. The *da capo* (from the beginning) form consists of two sections, the first being repeated after the second has been sung. Now, mere knowledge of the *da capo* form has never enabled anyone to write an interesting aria. But realization that such a form can be effective may help a composer to organize his musical thinking, and prevent him from floundering around in what may seem to his audiences an aimless fashion. This is exactly what happened in the early days of opera, when the invention of the aria was so important. An audience did not have to know how to construct an aria in order to recognize regularity and order in music, and to be grateful for them.

The same thing is true of the other elements of technique. Every pianist realizes that Beethoven achieved dramatic effects by sudden contrasts of loud and soft or by having his music race along and then come to a sudden stop, or by changing abruptly from a very slow passage to one at breakneck speed. Knowledge of what Beethoven did enlarged the range of musical composition, but in the hands of lesser men led to no great works.

Every student of opera knows how Rossini obtained many of his effects, and some critics have sneered at him for getting them too cheaply. For excitement, Rossini would have his orchestra play more and more rapidly, with additional instruments joining every few seconds, while the key of his melody gradually rose higher and higher. The trick is so simple that it too can be mastered by a tone-deaf composer or by a machine. But many of Rossini's rivals, who were far from tone deaf, could never do it in a way that would please an audience. Evidently Rossini had talent to go along with his tricks.

LE NOZZE DI FIGARO

DIE HOCHZEIT DES FIGARO

Eine comische Oper in vier Aufzügen

in Musik gesetzt

von

WOLFGANG AMADEUS MOZART

CLAVIER-AUSZUG

HAMBURG

Bey Iohann August Böhme.

Title page of original piano score, showing a scene from the first act of Mozart's opera, The Marriage of Figaro.

From the beginning, the composer's critical and creative abilities must work together. He must decide how large an orchestra to use, and what instruments to write for. The larger his orchestra, the more striking the effects he can produce. But does he want to astound his audience or move it? If the latter is his purpose, a small orchestra will often do. And there is the practical consideration that it is easier to produce an opera that calls for a small orchestra than an opera that demands a large one.

The possession of talent, technique, and critical sense is not enough. The real test is the composer's inspiration and his ability to produce exciting and interesting music for the one libretto he has chosen. The modern composer, especially, is not in any hurry.

Rossini wrote his *Barber of Seville* in thirteen days, and Donizetti wanted to know what took him so long. Handel required an additional day to compose the music for *Rinaldo,* and Mozart required as much as six weeks for *The Marriage of Figaro.* But in six weeks Wagner would very likely still be brooding over the possibilities of the libretto and would have done no more than the sketching of a few leading motives. For his own day, because of his involved method of composition, Wagner was a slow composer. However, it is also true that he used larger orchestras. In general, we may note that composers of one or two centuries ago wrote with more facility, with less worry about critical judgment, and possibly with more genius.

But many of the problems they faced were easier to solve. The average composer of the eighteenth century, busily tossing off a score in the usual four to six weeks, could always, if inspiration failed, lift music from one of his own previous operas. If his own operas were not worth borrowing from, he could choose a less well-known opera by some predecessor. He could do this because of the large number of operas being written, the impossibility of remembering them all, and the prevailing belief that arias were display pieces and not means of characterization. He usually had no feelings of guilt at having borrowed, certainly not if he borrowed from himself. When he was paid a hundred and fifty dollars per opera, and no royalties, the feeling of guilt was a luxury he could not afford.

The financial position of the composer improved in the nineteenth century. Rossini, in his short working career, became wealthy. By Verdi's time, the demand for new operas was so insistent that when Verdi stopped writing in discouragement at a failure, it was the management that urged him to keep on. He responded with *Nabucco,* a hit, and thus launched a successful career.

The financial position of the successful operatic composer contrasted sharply with that of the symphonic composer. Hector Berlioz, who was writing critical articles about music for the newspapers and journals of the early nineteenth century, describes vividly the position of the symphonic composer. He tells of having a dream in which he composed a symphony. On awakening, he remembered nearly the whole of the first movement, and was going to begin writing it down, when he reflected: "If I write this part I shall let myself be carried on to write the rest. . . . I may perhaps spend three or four months exclusively upon it. . . . Meantime I shall do no feuilletons [columns of music criticism] or next to none, and my income will suffer. When the symphony is finished I shall be weak enough to allow my copyist to copy it out, and thus immediately incur a debt of one thousand or twelve hundred francs. Once the parts are copied, I shall be harassed by the temptation to have the work performed; I shall give a concert in which, . . . the receipts will barely cover half the expenses . . ."

To make a sad story short, he never so much as began the symphony, and it was lost forever.

No wonder that Berlioz and the other musicians of his day were tempted to write opera, whether or not they had the special talent for it, since it was a form of musical composition that did not inevitably lead to poverty.

The financial position of the successful operatic composer remained good for the rest of the century, and it was not very difficult for a newcomer with talent to be successful. Gradually, however, the situation changed. The growing repertory of favorite old operas provided more and more competition for the newcomer's work. As opera companies learned to get along nicely with the works of Mozart, Wagner, Puccini, and other old reliables, they began to turn a more and more jaundiced eye on

Puccini, the composer of La Bohème, Tosca, Madama Butterfly, *and other operas, in his studio in Italy.*

new compositions. Why spend money on new scenery and extra time on learning and rehearsing unfamiliar parts for a new work that might be a total failure?

The great composers of previous days had their share of failures and learned that they were to be expected. The first performance of Rossini's *Barber* was hissed, but Rossini was not at all disturbed. Beethoven found the initial lack of success of *Fidelio* harder to swallow, but he worked on the opera again until he finally achieved a moderate success. Puccini's *La Bohème* and *Madama Butterfly,* and Bizet's *Carmen* had unsuccessful first nights, and then went on with relatively minor changes to become popular favorites.

Nowadays, however, an initial failure at a house like the Metropolitan or La Scala can be disastrous. For possibly two years the composer must drop all other work and devote himself to the writing of his opera. He must refuse such lucrative if uninspiring offers as the writing of television or movie music, and devote himself to his arias and trios and quartets, and to difficult orchestrations that will meet with merciless criticism. At the end of his two years he must have his work copied, and this is far more expensive than it was in the days of Berlioz. If, despite all the odds against him, the composer has his opera accepted by a large opera company, what can he expect?

Ordinarily he may expect a thousand dollars or so for a world premiere. If he is famous, he may expect as much as two thousand dollars. And very often, that is all. If his work is repeated later in the season, or at a different opera house, he may receive a few hundred dollars additional. Only in the most exceptional cases can he earn even a meager living by writing opera.

Recently, a few composers have received commissions to do operas, and have been partly subsidized in advance. But the number of subsidies is too small to change the situation materially.

All honor to the few brave souls who continue to write opera under the most difficult circumstances.

management 5

When librettist and composer have completed their work, their opera exists only as a score—an opera on paper. To bring it to life, one might think that only a few singers and an orchestra are needed. In fact, a large organization is required, composed of people most of whom never appear on stage or in the pit, and the three-hour performance of an opera that an audience sees and hears is the result of more than a year of their labor.

The first questions involved in putting on an opera must be answered by the management: what operas to stage, how to stage them, what singers to use. These are formidable problems, and today's management of a large opera company is a formidable affair. If you will look at the page of a Metropolitan Opera program which lists members of the administration, you will get an idea of how much there is to do and how many people it takes to do it. The general manager, who is in overall charge, is supported by two assistant managers, each of whom has his own assistants. He can also call on the services of a business and technical administrator, an artistic administrator, and a comptroller, who is in charge of financial affairs. Each of these gentlemen likewise has assistants. There are, in addition, a musical consultant, a legal counsel, a box office treasurer, and a company manager, not to speak of secretaries and other assistants. The entire management staff totals about thirty-two.

Why are so many people needed? The answer is that a company like the Metropolitan in New York, or La Scala in Milan, produces about twenty-five different operas each season, and the general manager faces the problem of crowding twenty-five years of preparation into a season of little more than half a year. An organization devoted to opera is therefore not a company in the sense that a play-producing group is a company. It is an organization that has at its disposal a stock of tenors, sopranos, and directors who are available when needed. Most of its parts are interchangeable, and when one of them breaks down, as when a tenor has laryngitis or a soprano a fit of temper, there is usually at least one spare ready.

Sometimes additional spares are needed, as in a famous performance of Wagner's *Tristan* at the Metropolitan, when the original tenor couldn't continue after Act I, the second tenor broke down in Act II, and a third tenor was needed to finish the performance, all playing against a single indomitable soprano.

The management of any large group deals with people and with material things. The management of an opera must concern itself with art as well. That is why its task is so extraordinarily difficult. It is not enough if the individuals who make up an opera company are happy in their work and temporarily satisfied with their salaries, if the sets are moved without confusion, and if everything takes place exactly on schedule in any one opera. Each performance must have musical and dramatic value, and the season as a whole must be a contribution to the cultural life of the country.

The need for maintaining musical and dramatic values and for the making of a cultural contribution have existed from the early days of opera, but in the seventeenth century many of the complications of present-day management's job did not exist.

In France, Lully was able both to compose his operas and to manage their production. Composer-managers were fairly common even through the nineteenth century, Wagner being among the most famous. Wagner and other composers, however, managed subsidized court operas, and were therefore not concerned with all the problems involved in attracting the public to a modern opera. The opera companies of Naples, Milan, and Paris, on the other hand, had to fill fairly large houses if they were to be financially successful, and the business aspects of management were difficult for a practicing composer to handle.

Nevertheless, the tradition of great composers as opera-house managers lasted into the twentieth century. By this time, however, the many duties of management were making it impossible for composers and conductors to administer the affairs of a large organization. Orchestras had grown larger, music had become more complex, new ways of staging and lighting had developed, carpenters and stagehands had begun to appreciate their own value, and had organized into unions with whom long negotiations were necessary.

Composers and conductors as managers were in many places replaced by administrators, men who knew a great deal about opera, but might not be able to compose a bar of music or play a single instrument. In 1908, the Board of Directors of the Metropolitan Opera chose as its new manager Giulio Gatti-Casazza, who had trained for a career in naval architecture. Gatti-Casazza entered the world of opera by following his father as director of the Municipal Theatre at Ferrara, Italy. Then he became director of La Scala, in Milan, before going on to the Metropolitan.

His successor at the Metropolitan, Edward Johnson, was the

only singer in its history to become manager. He is said to have shown excellent business sense, and was highly regarded by members of the company.

Johnson was succeeded in 1950 by Rudolf Bing, who had a background of concert and opera management in Germany, England, and Scotland.

In smaller opera companies, or in those with less ambitious production schedules, it is still possible for a man to combine management with artistic functions. In the Berlin Komische Oper, for instance, Walter Felsenstein very advantageously combines management with direction. As manager, he permits himself, as director, to stage an unlimited number of rehearsals. This makes it impossible for him to depend on visiting stars, whose rehearsal time is limited. Instead he retains the same chief singers from one production to another and decreases the number of productions, thus simplifying his work as manager.

You may get a clearer picture of the complications involved in dealing with the personnel of an opera company of today from this list of the number of individuals in different categories on the staff of the Metropolitan Opera. Other, smaller, opera companies would, of course, have smaller staffs.

Orchestra:	102	(plus about 15 extra)
Chorus:	78	(plus about 30 extra)
Ballet:	36	(plus about 8 extra)
Supers:	250	(approximately)
Porters, etc.:	45	
Musical and artistic staff:	128	
General staff:	32	
Engineers:	6	
Scenic workers:	6	
Wardrobe department:	26	

Ushers: 64
Stagehands: 105 (of whom 22 are employed all year round)

These seven hundred or so individuals, whose exact number varies from opera to opera and season to season, are organized in fourteen unions, from the International Brotherhood of Firemen, Oilers, and Maintenance Mechanics to the American Guild of Musical Artists.

The management must sign general contracts with each union, as well as individual contracts with conductors, singers, and other artists. Until the last contract is signed, there is no guarantee that the operas for the season will be given as scheduled, and work by designers and set builders is accordingly held up. In the past, several seasons have been canceled, and then scheduled again as management and unions reached agreement. But there is always the possibility that a season's schedule will be really canceled.

The opera company looks for ways of economizing, both in salaries and in equipment, while the unions insist that the economies should not take place at their expense. Questions of personnel also crop up. The management may claim that a certain trombonist is blowing too many wrong notes, and the union may counter that the management is trying to get rid of him for other reasons. The case may easily develop into a question of principle: shall the management have the right to hire and fire at will, or shall a man who has given much of his life to his work have job protection? The usual result is a compromise.

Satisfactory compromises, however, are not easy to find. Behind the manager stand the officers and board of directors of the opera association, along with their legal counsel, who realize that a decision on one point may set a precedent for similar decisions in cases yet to come up. Behind the local union stand its International Union and related unions, all aware that any contract with the nation's leading opera company may set a pattern for orchestras and opera groups elsewhere. As the argument grows hotter, therefore, a city or federal mediator may enter the picture, hoping to induce both sides to make concessions in order to keep the opera going.

Though a great deal of his time is taken up in dealing with personnel and in settling quarrels between conductors and singers, or directors and dancers, the real test of a manager's ability comes when he chooses his assistants. Because he cannot attend to more than a fraction of the details of management himself, he must hire people who can do everything as he wants it done—people who can see to it that singers are reached and signed to contracts in time, that sets are ordered and built, that repairs are made, rehearsals properly scheduled.

His conductors, stage directors, stage managers, choreographers (dance arrangers), and all the others must have a high degree of professional skill and be able to do an excellent job, with little time to do it in. These people may choose their own subordinates—the conductors and musical director, for instance, selecting new members of the orchestra—but the manager, if he wishes, has a say about this too.

In the early days of opera the duties of the opera manager included looking for new composers and ordering a number of new operas from them each season. The modern opera manager still has that duty. He is wary, however, of commissioning new operas, knowing that each new work will cost him thousands of dollars that will have to be chalked up to experience and art, since he cannot expect enough financial return to meet the expense.

Instead of looking for new composers, the modern opera manager is likely to spend his time looking for new conductors and singers. The Metropolitan management covers a good part of Europe each year in its search for new performing talent, spotting new singers as they acquire experience, and signing up those who are thought ready to perform in a first-class opera company. Opera is like baseball in its use of a scouting system.

Once he has his assistants and his artists, most of a manager's time is taken up with the planning of the next season's operas. Each opera is scheduled at least one and sometimes two seasons in advance. The list for the entire coming year is drawn up on the basis of a set of requirements which are individually simple, but complicated and often conflicting when taken as a whole. There are more than a hundred popular operas to choose from, several hundred not so well known but still popular, and many that were once popular and may be welcomed if occasionally revived.

The new year's repertory must differ from that of the previous year, or the management will be accused of lack of imagination. It must have some old favorites, or habitual opera-goers will be disappointed. *Aida, Carmen,* and *Cavalleria Rusticana,* to name but a few, are old standbys in almost every country; Mozart must be included, and so must Verdi, Wagner, Puccini, and one or two others. And a company with a far-seeing management presents a new work every few seasons, or oftener if good ones come along, to encourage contemporary talent.

The first, tentative, selection is thus made on the basis of the management's knowledge of the operas that will continue to attract large audiences and still maintain a high cultural level. Then consideration is given to the amount of money that is available for new operas or for old operas which are to be produced in a new way. Although an opera company is not expected to

The finale of Cavalleria Rusticana *by Mascagni*

make money, management cannot afford to have it lose too much. The selection will not be the same in different countries or even in various parts of one country.

Now comes the delicate question of the singers and conductors who will be at the company's disposal. Because great conductors and singers are rarely under exclusive contract to one company for an entire season, the scheduling of their performance depends on their availability at the proper time. Contracts for the services of all major artists are therefore signed far in advance, and if the necessary singers cannot be obtained for the right time, some operas may have to be stricken from the list.

As any company that plays for a full season has at least a hundred soloists, we may appreciate the complexities of preparing a schedule. Although twenty-five operas may be scheduled, there will be perhaps a hundred and fifty performances, and at each one different artists will take some of the leading roles.

The juggling of operas, dates, and casts of singers is so difficult that the task may some day be given over to some agency less liable to headache than the human brain—possibly an electronic computer. We say this in all seriousness, for computers have already been used in scheduling, and they can take account of such human factors as the popularity of certain singers and operas if instructed to do so.

We have noted that singers and directors are to some extent interchangeable. Opera managers would be delighted if one soprano could always be replaced by another, but unfortunately this cannot be done. A few individuals can range over the entire operatic repertory. But the average singer's roles are limited by his background and training as well as by his voice. A soprano who specializes in Italian opera may sing French roles that lie within her vocal range, but may be unable to manage a Wagnerian heroine. A Wagnerian soprano may sing Richard Strauss, but will sometimes be a bit too vigorous for *Madama Butterfly.*

Once the schedule has been arranged, only a minimum of preparation is needed for old productions. Their scenery is ready and the manner of staging them has been decided. Little need be done until actual rehearsals begin. Sometimes, however, the production is *too* old. Then the management faces a number of problems. To illustrate them, let us take one opera and follow its progress from scheduling to the point where rehearsals are ready to begin. (Later we shall follow it through rehearsals to the first performance.)

Aïda, by Giuseppe Verdi, has been a great favorite since its premiere in 1871 in Cairo, Egypt, and is in the active repertory of every opera house in Europe and the Western Hemisphere. The action takes place in ancient Egypt, and the story tells of the love and death of Aïda, an Ethiopian princess who is a slave

A scene from a production of Aïda *by Verdi at the Metropolitan Opera House many years ago. The set, a model of tinseled vulgarity, must have seemed the last word in lavishness to its audiences.*

at the court of the Egyptian Pharoah. As a theatrical spectacle, it is unparalleled in splendor. In many places, the victory procession of the Pharoah's army is seized upon as an excuse to bring a virtual Noah's Ark on stage, the animals in the procession including every beast from the domestic horse to the once exotic elephant.

Having decided that its budget will stand the strain, and that everything about *Aïda,* from scenery to staging, requires renovation, the management must make its casting decisions. In the spring or early summer before the new season begins, a conductor is chosen and at least two sopranos are selected to sing the heroine's role. Two sets of soloists are scheduled for each of the other

A more recent production of Aïda. *The set is simpler, more stylized, and permits the eyes to focus on the performers. Different stage levels are utilized to allow for more interesting staging.*

roles. In case of illness or other emergency, the additional singers under contract for other operas will probably be happy to do *Aïda* as well.

Only after the musical choices are made is the stage director selected and assignments given to stage and costume designers, and to the choreographer. In an opera where ballet dancers may have to compete with elephants, it might seem that dancing was of secondary importance, but ballet is an important part of *Aïda* and cannot be neglected.

Now comes an apparently endless series of pre-season conferences. Before any detailed work is done, the director, designer, and conductor must iron out any conflicts in artistic approach.

Among these three, the conductor has the final word. He has overall authority at the conferences, and he will continue to have it at rehearsals and performances. Shall the story be emphasized more than it has been in past productions, shall the sets be simpler and more stylized, shall there be more stage action, shall the singers be called upon to do more acting than usual, shall the spectacles be made more or less spectacular? How shall the ballet be integrated into the performances?

The director, especially if most of his work has been in non-musical theatre, wants to emphasize stage action and dancing, wants the sets to provide plenty of room for dancers and chorus to move around in. The stage designer will agree, but he also wants his sets to have an importance of their own. The conductor wants, above all, to make sure that nothing in the production interferes with the effect the music will create.

Not until September, when all the discussions and all the preparatory work have been completed, do the first rehearsal calls go out and the personnel of the company, including the chorus, orchestra, ballet, and administrative and technical staffs report to the opera house.

Before seeing how rehearsals take place, we shall meet some of the artists and other people who are needed for the production. In the meantime, the management is finishing the previous season, and trying to tally its victories and defeats. What sort of season was it?

A century ago, Verdi could advise opera managers to watch the box office and not the critics' reviews, and in those days this was a sensible criterion, for many opera companies expected to make a profit. For small professional opera companies and for amateur groups, Verdi's advice remains valid. These companies continually struggle to attract the public, and their success can be measured only by counting the box office receipts.

For companies like the Metropolitan, Verdi's method of judgment is obsolete. The Metropolitan Opera House is always at least ninety percent full, and by that criterion is invariably successful. But it also invariably loses money, and by this latter criterion is a failure.

The only remaining standard is the artistic one, and that cannot always be judged by attendance. Many people have season tickets and attend regularly whether or not they like the particular opera. There will always be a certain portion of the audience at the Metropolitan who go merely to be seen. On the other hand, the popularity of certain operas can be judged by the demand for seats not taken by subscription, but the management, although it likes its operas to be popular, does not confuse popularity with artistic success. It seeks—and sometimes, even if it does not seek, it hears—the opinions of singers, conductors, newspaper and magazine critics, officers of the Metropolitan Opera Association, members of the Board of Directors, and its subscribers and visitors.

In the long run, the success or failure of an opera season, and of the man chiefly responsible for it—the manager himself—is judged by a number of factors. How smoothly did things run? How well did the manager get along with his colleagues? Was the Board of Directors happy? Were the critical reviews generally favorable? How enthusiastic were the audiences? Was the deficit larger or smaller than in previous years?

In any given season, it is no wonder that final judgments differ considerably from one person to the next, and that the manager is not quite sure where he stands.

No specific training can be suggested for a management job, except to learn everything possible about the operas, and about the functioning of an opera company, and to work in different kinds of jobs in different companies.

the conductor 6

MOST PEOPLE THINK of an opera conductor as a thorough musician dedicated to his art. He is that, of course, and much more. Rather surprisingly, he is a tough, hard-boiled, quick-thinking individual who, like the hero of a Western, is ready for trouble at all times. Unlike the hero, the conductor usually does not pack a gun, although he will if the occasion warrants. In 1891, when Wagner's *Lohengrin* was being given at the Paris Opéra, the conductor, Charles Lamoureux, did carry a pistol, for the Parisian opera-goers had not forgotten the Franco-Prussian war of 1870, and Wagner was a hated German. Fortunately, nothing more serious happened than the throwing of a stink bomb.

American conductors usually do not expect trouble from the audience, but conductors all over the world know that anything can happen on stage. A curtain may rise or fall at the wrong time, a trap door refuse to open, a singer come in on the wrong note, a dancer take a tumble. The conductor must be ready to cover up mistakes when possible and to carry on under all circumstances.

How does the conductor receive his training? Usually he starts to study music without the slightest idea that he will ever stand in front of an orchestra with a baton. Most often he begins by studying the piano, although Toscanini was a cellist, and Serge Koussevitzky, famous as an orchestral conductor, was a double bass player. Piano study gets the student used to playing many notes at a time—and it should also get him used to listening to them if he expects to become a musician. The disadvantage is that the pitch produced depends not on the player's ear but on the way the piano is tuned. This is beyond his control, and a badly tuned piano may accustom the student to accept off-pitch sounds. The cellist, or violinist, or other string player has to produce his own pitch, but not until he joins a chamber group or orchestra is he faced with the problem of determining how his thread of melody fuses with a larger mass of sound.

These difficulties, serious for inferior musicians, are easily overcome by anyone who has a genuine ability to conduct. But there are no courses in conducting for ten- or twelve-year-old music students (although an occasional young prodigy will lead an orchestra with surprising skill). Nor are such courses needed. What is important is the acquiring by the student of a thorough musical training.

By the time he is of college age, the student will be able to take courses in conducting at one or two of the best music schools in the United States. Before he is allowed to take such a course, he must show that he has a good ear, can play at least one instrument well, and has a fair knowledge of others. He must be well trained in harmony, know something about musical composition, and have the necessary qualities of character to become a conductor.

The taking of such a course guarantees nothing so far as a career is concerned, and the greatest of conductors have had no formal lessons in conducting. But the student may have a chance to lead an orchestra and learn how it feels to stand before a body of musicians and try to make them carry out his musical ideas.

The man who hopes to become a good conductor must know, before he is twenty, more music than the average professional musician learns in a lifetime. His actual musical experience cannot, of course, be as great as that of a sixty-year-old violinist. But he must have an ear sharp enough to analyze the sounds he has heard, unusual ability to concentrate, and a memory for music so good that on one reading of the score he can grasp the meaning of a new composition and recall it fairly well. His memory need not be perfect. Very few conductors conduct as Toscanini did, without a score, and some who do would be better off with the music before them. But the score must have been mastered beforehand, and during an actual performance usually serves merely as a guide, for no man can read ten or twenty lines of complicated music as rapidly as an orchestra can play them. The conductor must hear the hundreds of notes that an orchestra may toss off in a second, but he need not follow each one on the printed page.

Once the would-be conductor has the necessary training, what then? At this point comes the test of character: he must be able to accept continual disappointment and discouragement. In the United States, certainly, few orchestras are looking for conductors, and those willing to try out inexperienced conductors are non-existent. The would-be conductor must usually make one of several different choices. He may join an orchestra, playing the instrument in which he specialized, and hope that as a result of his experience, opportunities to conduct will open up.

He may start a small orchestra of his own. For a student this is usually out of the question, unless he is willing to accept unskilled amateurs, or has enough money to pay professional musicians out of his own pocket, as Sir Thomas Beecham did at first.

Finally, he may try to get a position as assistant with a well-established orchestra (the New York Philharmonic has three

A stage rehearsal of Lohengrin *by Wagner at the Metropolitan. Note the prompter, half out of his box, following the score.*

such assistants) or with an opera company (the Metropolitan Opera has a number of conductors and assistants). This is the choice most would-be conductors would make, but it is difficult to get these positions, and even after he has one, he may have to wait for years to show what he can do.

Assistant opera conductors, known as répetiteurs, help in rehearsing singers and choruses, give the beat to groups of singers and musicians who cannot see the conductor (when they are singing offstage, for example), and generally take care of the thousand and one musical details that the conductor cannot attend to himself.

Assistants usually act as prompters: that is, one of them will sit in the prompter's box at the front of the stage, giving the first word of every aria or every line to a singer during a performance, or all the words if the singer has suffered a serious lapse of memory. He follows the conductor's beat with a mirror and passes it on to the singers, who may be too nearsighted to see the conductor in the pit. Other assistants stand in the wings, and repeat the words of the arias to singers about to make their entrances, and give them the pitch from pitchpipes.

The assistants are talented men with little chance to use their talents fully. Their work is to carry out the conductor's musical ideas and not their own. They may think he is taking an aria too slowly, but they pass on the beat that he gives them. They may disagree violently with his interpretation of a duet, but they rehearse their singers as he wishes. Any other method of working would lead to serious confusion.

Inevitably, these bright young men, as they become older, developing their talents to a limited extent while losing their youth, regard the conductor with some envy, and feel that with a bit of luck they could take his place. In many cases they are right. Some luck is needed to become a conductor, as it is needed to become an opera singer or orchestral musician. But luck alone never made a conductor—even a bad one.

The average assistant conductor is forced to wait year after year for the conductor and all the assistants who are ahead of him in rank to get sick one at a time before he has his big chance.

The tragedy of this situation is that when he does get his chance he may fail to shine, purely for lack of experience, and sink back hopelessly into his usual rut. For every Toscanini who, during an emergency, leaves his instrument for the conductor's podium and becomes a sensation, there are a dozen John Smiths who are commended by the critics and public for having done a competent, workmanlike job, and then sink again into obscurity.

In Europe, with its numerous orchestras and opera houses, good and bad, a young conductor has the chance to gain experience, which is the one thing he needs beyond native talent and training. That is why so many of our best conductors have been European.

With experience comes not only the confidence that arises from doing the same thing again and again, but an even greater knowledge of music and a familiarity with all the accidents that can affect a performance. Experience also provides something that no school can give: the realization that a conductor must stand on his own feet, that no teacher is nearby to correct mistakes. Mistakes are more serious in a conductor, who stands alone, than in a performer, who is surrounded by fellow performers. The young conductor cannot help making them, and he must learn to suffer the consequences.

Just as he needs to acquire experience in conducting, he must also acquire experience in leading men. He must win their respect for his knowledge and for his fairness in treating them. He must learn how to steer a middle course between extreme strictness, which arouses resentment, and the laxity which they regard as a sign of weakness and indecision.

Once he has passed all these dangers, has had his chance, and has succeeded, what is his reward? First of all, he has the satisfaction of performing on the most magnificent musical instrument yet invented—an opera company. Playing one instrument in the orchestra has not satisfied him. That is why he became a conductor. He knows that if he can reach the top, his importance to the success of an opera will be recognized, if not by the public, at least by musicians and management. The recognition brings him honor and, of course, money. A first-rate conductor in this country may earn thirty to fifty thousand dollars a year, depending on the number of works he is willing to conduct, the number of recordings he makes, and so on. If he is at the peak of his popularity, he may earn even more.

A conductor's job would seem to call for the qualities of a musical superman. When we consider the talent and determination he has shown, and the odds he has had to fight against, we can hardly consider him overpaid.

Few realize that it is the conductor more than any other individual who decides what kind of performance the public will hear. If he is unsure of the music or himself, the singing as well as the orchestral playing will suffer, not to speak of the audience. If he has an unconventional or eccentric idea of the opera's meaning, his listeners will be shocked by the unfamiliar sound of familiar music. They may or may not like it, but they will certainly not get what most of them expected.

The conductor can destroy the effect of an orchestral performance by emphazing what the composer wanted to subdue; he can drown out a tenor by blasts from his wind instruments; he can ruin an aria by taking the music at so fast a clip that no soprano can keep up. He can go to the other extreme of playing so softly that a soloist's voice seems to stand naked and alone, unsupported by the harmonies it needs, or he may set so slow a pace that singer and audience feel they will die of boredom before an aria is completed.

From time to time a conductor commits one or other of these crimes, but the public is rarely aware of them. It knows merely that the singer sang well or badly, and almost always assumes that the cause lay in the singer alone.

The conductor of an opera in a reputable company is not often guilty of ruining a performance completely. But bad or indifferent performances *are* given in the best opera houses, and if any single individual is to blame, it is probably the conductor. The opera looks and sounds the way he wants it to look and sound. He cannot plead as an excuse that he couldn't control his orchestra or singers, any more than a pianist can plead that he could not control his fingers.

It is true that a young and comparatively inexperienced conductor will have his troubles. Both instrumentalists and singers will take advantage of him, and the management may fail to support his authority. If he is tough-minded enough, and is sure of his ground musically and dramatically, he will get the performers to do as he wishes, although he will certainly suffer while doing so.

If they cannot, or say they cannot, do as he directs, he must drill them, as Toscanini mercilessly drilled his unhappy singers and players, and if after rehearsal they still cannot sing as he wishes, he usually has no excuse, at any rate not if he himself had a hand in choosing them.

In most opera houses, once the conductor is chosen, he has at least formal authority over singers, instrumentalists, stage director, assistant conductors, and every other artist connected with that opera. He may have difficulties with a famous singer, but if he is of sufficient stature as a conductor he will usually get his way. Most singers are not given to excited outbursts. Displays of temperament were common enough fifty years ago, but there is little time or patience for them now.

Paradoxically, one of the reasons the conductor may be blamed for bad performances is that he has accustomed us, in the last half century or so, to such good ones. Some aged members of audiences, and a few critics, talk wistfully of the good old days of opera, when singers had golden voices and could really sing. Of this we shall have more to say later. But here let us note that no one with musical taste pretends that performances in general were better a half century ago or a century ago than they are now. The contrary is true. Low standards were tolerated then that would not be tolerated now. One opera conductor, for instance, could not follow an orchestral score with any ease, but had to learn the music from a piano arrangement. It would be practically impossible nowadays for such a man to become a conductor in even a poor opera house.

For the change that has taken place, a few great conductors are largely responsible. Present-day conductors must pay the penalty by having their own work compared with the best.

In Mozart's day, and for a decade or two after, there was no conductor for the opera as a whole. The orchestra was under the control of the concert master, the leader of the first violins, while activities on stage were supervised by a *kapellmeister* (choir master), usually the composer himself. The composer sat at a harpsichord or piano, strummed chords to accompany the dry recitatives, gave cues to the singers, and set the proper tempo for each part of the opera. At the Paris Opéra and a few other places, an assistant beat time by pounding a large staff on the floor. The baton that we are familiar with was not introduced until the middle of the nineteenth century.

As the orchestra grew, both in size and in importance to the opera, its control could no longer be relegated to some subordinate, and the composer took over complete musical direction. In doing so, he acquired new headaches. Remember that one of the composer's duties was to struggle with the singers, who had once thought that the opera was written merely to display their voices. On taking over leadership of the orchestra as well, the composer found himself dealing with temperamental instrumentalists, who regarded the entire performance as an opportunity for them to display their virtuosity on the instrument they played. By enlarging the orchestra and by giving it more and better music to play the composer had created more interesting operas, and at the same time added to his own troubles.

Erich Leinsdorf conducting a rehearsal of the Metropolitan Opera orchestra in a studio of the opera house.

The composer as conductor was, however, only a passing phase in opera. As opera became "grand," as the number of singers and performers continued to grow, the burden became intolerable. Parts had to be written for the increased number of performers, and composition of an opera took more and more time. So did the selection of singers and instrumentalists, the direction, and the rehearsal.

Moreover, as time went on, it became clear that the best composers were not necessarily the best conductors. There have been striking exceptions in the past, but in our own day, at least, none of the renowned conductors is highly regarded as a composer, nor are the composers among the leading conductors. The composer may be expected to know best how he wants his own music to sound. All the other advantages lie on the side of the conductor. The two men therefore play separate roles in most modern opera.

The opera conductor must have the imagination to exploit possibilities the composer has written into the score, but need not and should not be creative in the same way. As indicated before, the conductor does need an extremely sharp ear, and a thorough and well-rounded musical training. He must know when any detail has gone wrong, and he must know how to set it right. He must know what can be done with human voices of different kinds and with all the instruments of his orchestra. And he must have had experience with many operas, possibly as an assistant at first, so that he is familiar with every detail of a performance, and knows what to do in any of the innumerable cases where something can go wrong.

The conductor must have the ability to give orders and see that they are carried out, without causing resentment, and must, of course, have the authority to do so. Musicians have nothing but contempt for any one who gives orders for the pleasure of doing so, without knowing what he wants to achieve. Toscanini was a man who demanded perfection and drove his orchestra and singers to exhaustion in order to get it, with the result that he was often regarded as a tyrant. Any other conductor who used the same tactics might have touched off a revolt. But there was never more than a momentary rebellion against Toscanini, because his musicians realized that his tyranny arose from a deep love and knowledge of music.

His ear was incredible. There are endless stories about him, but one, of which there are many versions, will typify his qualities: Once, when the orchestra was going full blast, and the average listener would have been conscious only of a blended mass of sound, he stopped a rehearsal and shouted at a violinist, "Stupido! You play B flat when the score says B natural!"

The violinist, startled at being singled out from his comfortable obscurity among a dozen other violinists all sawing away at the same notes, looked at his music. "I'm sorry, Maestro," he said apologetically, "but I've always played B flat. It says B flat in the score."

"It cannot say B flat. Show me where it says B flat."

"Here," said the nervous violinist, and pointed to the disputed note.

The conductor looked, and snorted. "Idiot!" he shouted. "The note is B. All these years you have been playing a fly-speck!"

A man with so keen an ear, so splendid a musical talent, and so deadly a memory for every note of a vast orchestral score does not come along in every generation. As a matter of fact, the average orchestral player is rather pleased that his conductor is no Toscanini. Even though the performance may suffer slightly, a conductor who does not hear or at least not comment upon *every* mistake creates less strain.

The authority a conductor wields thus depends on his musical ability, his executive ability, his experience, and the opposing authority of a few of his colleagues. If he is a great musician and a great man as well, he may rule with an authority that kings might envy.

the singers 7

WHEN NICCOLÒ PORPORA, the great singing teacher of the early eighteenth century, received one particularly promising pupil, Caffarelli, he was supposed to have given the earnest student a page of exercises and had him practice it for five years. At the end of that time he is reported to have said, "I have taught you all I can. Go, you are now the greatest singer in Europe."

This fable must have been believed by many people, or it would not have been repeated for two centuries. Nevertheless, we can be sure it had little basis in fact. Porpora, whatever his eccentricities—and no teacher of singing is without them—was extremely successful, and the endless repetition of a single exercise would hardly produce a great singer. Porpora may have had his pupil return to the same exercise now and then over a period of five years to note the improvement in his technique. Or he may have given Caffarelli a set of warming-up exercises that the singer used throughout his career.

About no group of artists have so many incredible stories been believed as about singers. Some of these stories have a bit of truth in them, but a good many are pure nonsense. Among these are stories intended to prove what may be called superstitions about singers and singing:

"Great singers are stupid." This is a favorite statement of those who like only instrumental music and of those who hate music altogether. It is a myth that has been kept alive by conductors and composers, many of whom regard singers as their natural enemies. It was a composer-conductor who said, "A tenor is not a man but a disease."

"There are no more great voices. The last one died with Caruso." This is a repeated lament of aging critics, both amateur and professional.

"The secret of being a great singer is the way you breathe," or "the way you place your voice,"—whatever that means—or "the way you control the muscles of your throat," or "the practice of special vocal exercises" so powerful and so secret that they are known only by one teacher, his pupils, and their neighbors in the next block. These are among the many treasured beliefs of some singing teachers and their students. George Bernard Shaw commented that in his day, seventy-five years ago, every singing teacher in London had the one infallible method of instruction and was certain that every other teacher was a fraud.

The origin of these superstitions about singing go back in musical history to the time when singers were the gods of opera. They revelled in the use of their power, just as if they had been politicians, merchants, ship captains, or movie stars. In the eighteenth century, particularly, they were the darlings of the audience. No wonder they behaved temperamentally. They made many enemies, and all the foolish things they did were widely publicized. When their power was curbed by Gluck and his successors, they behaved more sensibly, but by then the damage had been done. Remember that they ruled opera for more than two centuries, time enough for many malicious stories about them to become rampant.

The average singer, far from being a stupid individual who has nothing in his favor but the beautiful voice that nature gave him, and for which he deserves no credit, is a determined and able person. He may be vain and childish, but he is hardly likely to be unintelligent. The story of Marcella Sembrich, for instance, illustrates rather well the nature of that supposedly empty-headed creature, the soprano.

Sembrich was born (as Praxede Marcelline Kochanska) in Poland in 1858, the daughter of a street violinist who played for the coins people tossed him. As a child, she, too, learned to play the violin and also earned her living by playing it. Later she studied violin and piano in Vienna, where she married her violin teacher. When she played and sang before Franz Liszt, the greatest pianist of his generation, and a great composer as well, the old man suggested that she had a fine voice and that her true career lay in singing. Liszt's own experience with singers had begun at an early age. He had written an opera while still a boy, and had it produced in 1825, when he was fourteen, at the Paris Opéra.

At that time Sembrich knew little about singing and had no money for lessons. But Liszt's suggestion inspired her, and she became an accompanist for a famous voice teacher. She listened carefully as he instructed his students, and tried to put into practice what he taught. When an opportunity arose for her to sing in Athens, at a second-rate opera house which other sopranos disdained, she did not hesitate. She made her debut in 1877, and after that there was no stopping her. She became one of the famous singers of her day, and sang in concerts until 1924, eleven years before her death.

Sembrich had an unusual ability to learn from other singers without formal instruction. Note, however, that she had an excellent musical background, and a fine ear.

How does the average person become a singer, how do young men and women who do not come to the attention of a great musician know whether they have the talent to rise in so difficult a profession? And how, if they are going to learn from others, whether formally or not, can they choose the right teacher?

Often a child of six can profitably study music, but it is foolhardy for any one, especially a boy, to begin training for a career in singing before his voice has changed. The singer's range and the quality of his voice as well may be unpredictably altered. Girl's voices may drop only two or three tones during adolescence, but boys' voices may change as much as or more than an octave, with great individual variations. Caruso's voice was supposed to have changed only from alto to tenor, while Chaliapin's dropped all the way from boy soprano to bass. Moreover, a pleasing child's voice may turn into a quite ordinary adult voice or vice versa, and it is foolish to plan for a career as a singer unless the voice, after it has changed, is of good quality.

A good voice is of course indispensable for any one who hopes to sing in opera, but most people forget that it is not the only natural gift needed. Opera makes strenuous physical demands, and no one in frail health has a ghost of a chance. More important, the best voice is useless without an excellent ear. Indeed, one prominent teacher and coach ranks a keen musical ear above a fine voice as the first requirement. The singer must be able to reproduce with accuracy musical sounds that differ subtly in pitch, quality, and intensity. If he has a good ear to start with, it can be improved by training, just as a good voice can, but if he lacks one his case as a singer is hopeless. Many an unfortunate student with a pleasing voice has been scolded, screamed at, and denounced as stupid by frustrated teachers and by his parents because of his inability to sing on pitch. They fail to realize that what he cannot hear, he cannot possibly sing.

Given a good voice, a good ear, a healthy body, and reasonably good looks, where and how can the student find a teacher who will train him to make the best use of his gifts?

Here we are on touchy ground. It may comfort the parent or pupil who cannot tell a good teacher from a bad one to know that every head of a great music school faces the same problems. Shall he choose Giovanni Rossi, who advertises himself truthfully as the teacher of a famous tenor, or Johannes Schmidt, who can boast that he has coached a Wagnerian soprano? Rossi and Schmidt may have been only one of the numerous teachers each of these stars has had, and no one knows (possibly not even the singers themselves) whether they helped or hindered the operatic careers of their pupils. Franco Corelli, Metropolitan Opera tenor, decided that most teachers were harmful, and taught himself by listening to records of great singers. There are dangers in this method as well, and most musicians are strongly against it. A singer usually resorts to it in desperation, as Corelli did, after he has been exposed to the conflicting theories of different teachers.

What then does the head of a music school do? First of all, he goes into the musical background of the teacher. With whom did he himself study, and for how long? Does he know music, theory, singing, and opera? Can he play the piano musically, can he sing well? Who are his pupils, and at what stage of their careers has he taught them? Even if the answers seem satisfactory, they do not solve the problem. Among several rivals for the position, one will have better training, another a better teaching record, and a third a better personality. But all records are slightly misleading, and all short-range judgments of personality and character may be faulty. One other question is asked: does anyone know anything unfavorable about the prospective teacher? The answer is usually, "Yes," for rare is the teacher who has no enemies. When all the unpleasant things have been said about all the applicants, the one with the least to his discredit is likely to get the job.

The important questions include many that the ordinary person in search of a teacher does not ask and many, the answers to which, he cannot evaluate. Nevertheless, for a parent or beginner forced to rely on his own judgment there are hints that may prove useful.

Try to find out about a teacher's general background. In general, the good teacher is a good musician. It does not necessarily work the other way, however. Some people know music well and cannot teach, while others are great singers and cannot tell their pupils how to sing. But a man who is not a good musician is rarely a good teacher of music.

A teacher should have an excellent ear, considerable experience with the human voice, and a knowledge of what it can do at different stages of development. Unfortunately, in order to judge these qualities, you should have them yourself, so young singers or their parents or guardians are rarely in a position to draw accurate conclusions about the teacher's ability.

Avoid a teacher who leans heavily on supposedly "scientific" theories about voice production or breathing. Beautiful sounds cannot yet be produced by scientific methods. Machines can be constructed that will produce the sounds of speech and that will also sing. But these machines will need a tremendous amount of practice before they are ready to give concerts.

From infancy on we learn to speak by ear—by hearing and imitating the speech of others—with no knowledge of the muscles and organs by which sound is produced. Only those who are born deaf must learn to speak by conscious muscular control. Their speech is odd and difficult to understand, and even though they can learn to raise and lower the pitch of their voices in an imitation of singing, they cannot produce a recognizable tune.

Lips, tongue, and throat all help to produce the sounds of speech, but mere imitation of lip or tongue movements, for example, although it may result in improved enunciation, does not lead to the production of beautiful tones. For that matter, professional ventriloquists, moving their lips hardly at all, can speak clearly enough. Some teachers place a great deal of emphasis on "proper" breathing. Studies of prominent singers have shown that they all used different methods of breathing. "Proper" breathing, therefore, is simply breathing that fills the lungs with enough air at the right time.

The unscientific approach of those who believe they have found the one scientific method of teaching becomes clearer when we compare them with each other. Each teacher stands firmly opposed to his competitors, and denounces them as ignorant and harmful. In fact, we are all ignorant of the fine details involved in sound production not only by the human voice but even by orchestral instruments. Physicists have been studying musical instruments for many years, but they have yet to produce violins with as fine a tone as those Stradivarius made two and a half centuries ago without benefit of science. The vocal organs of a man are more complicated than the strings and body of a violin, and if physiologists and physicists were allowed to operate on vocal cords as they pleased, it is highly doubtful that they could produce one singer in ten thousand with the voice of a second-rate tenor.

There would be no more harm in a teacher's having incorrect theories of voice production than there would be in his believing that the earth was flat, if these theories did not lead to neglect of genuine musical training and to emphasis on methods that only increase the tension of the pupil. To make a pupil overly conscious of the way he breathes while singing is to do what the ant did when she asked the centipede to show her which of his hundred legs he moved first. The centipede stood paralyzed because he had never thought about it and was afraid he would make the wrong move. The pupil who is ordered to sing "from the chest," or is told "don't make your voice so dry," does not know how to obey these orders.

It does no good to tell such a pupil not to be tense, or even to give exercises to relieve tension. The best way to prevent tension is to center the pupil's attention on the music and on the sounds he is trying to produce instead of on his own muscles and mental condition.

It should be said, however, that although an appalling number of teachers are incompetent, and many harm their pupils by developing bad habits of singing or by wasting their time, there are few outright frauds and quacks. Many talk nonsense, but it is a nonsense in which they believe sincerely.

A good teacher will assess the quality of a new pupil's voice, note any faults that can be corrected, and find out what the pupil's range is. Many young singers strain their voices in an attempt to produce tones too high or too low for them. Some are tenors and try to sing baritone, and vice versa. The usual ranges for the common classifications are:

Bass: D or E just below the bass clef, and up two octaves.

Baritone: G, the lowest line of the bass clef, and up two octaves.

Tenor: B flat (second line of bass clef) and up two octaves.

Contralto: An octave below middle C to an octave above.

Alto: E below middle C and up two octaves.

Mezzo-soprano: G below middle C and up two octaves.

Soprano: B flat just below middle C and up two octaves.

Some teachers have slightly different ideas of what the ranges are. They will be less demanding for a contralto, allowing her to cut out a few notes from the top and bottom of the range listed here. They may insist that a true soprano starts from middle C and goes up two octaves. Composers too have their own ideas and may write notes too high for the average operatic soprano or too low for the baritone, although the parts call for soprano or baritone respectively. Nature, of course, does not classify singers in accordance with the beliefs of teachers or composers, and many voices will fall into intermediate classes. Although a professional singer is usually expected to have a range of at least two octaves, some, such as the coloratura soprano, are expected to have a greater range, up to F above the high C of the ordinary soprano. A singer who can sing the bottom notes of the bass range as well as the top notes of the baritone may call himself a bass-baritone. On the other hand, he may also give himself the same title if he can sing at neither extreme range.

It is harmful for a young singer to try to increase his range by singing at pitches that strain his voice. Very often a slight increase in range comes as the singer becomes more mature, and an improvement of quality may accompany it. A professional singer who has not utilized the full extent of his voice for years, may discover, after a career as a baritone, for example, that he can handle high notes sucessfully, and embark on a new career as a tenor.

In general, a wise teacher will train his pupil's ear to the utmost and allow him to sing in the way that is most natural and comfortable for him. The teacher will not ask the pupil to imitate his own mannerisms nor those of a famous singer. The violin, the viola, the cello, and the double bass are all string instruments of the same family, and the tone of each is produced by scraping a bow across strings, but the technique of drawing the bow is different for each. For that matter, Heifetz and Isaac Stern move their bow arm differently while playing the violin. Teacher and pupil should concentrate on essentials; that is, on the sounds produced, not on the tilt of the elbow of a violinist or the head of a singer.

The young man or woman who wants to sing in opera must be more than a singer. There was a time when inability to act did not matter. It matters now, and acting lessons have become part of the operatic singer's training. Some singers take their lessons very seriously indeed, and study the famous Stanislavsky method of acting, or some variation of it. Lessons in language, beginning with English, and including Italian, as well as French and German are indispensable.

The operatic hopeful is advised not to start with the singing of opera. Modern works, especially, are full of complicated music and require great vocal skill. The young singer should see opera and listen to recordings, without attempting to master the music. If he wants to try his voice on an aria, he might start with one from a seventeenth- or early eighteenth-century opera, which, as written, may be excellent practice. In actual performance, many of the old arias were sung with vocal embroidery that required the highest skill.

Once a student has the ability to sing difficult music (and his teacher must be the judge of this), it is time enough to acquire an operatic repertory. But a repertory is not learned quickly. The mastery of even a single role is not easy, and can be done in a reasonable length of time only by the singer who, in addition to being a good musician, is also blessed with a good memory. We read occasionally of understudies who got their first chance at an actual performance by taking the place of a scheduled singer who had fallen ill. As the operas of Verdi, for example, are frequently given, and each may contain more than a single part for soprano, it is clear that a soprano who really wants to be prepared had better master all the soprano roles for each opera.

Later on, as a singer who consistently receives the leading role, she may let herself forget the secondary parts, but ordinarily she must be ready to sing in any one of twenty operas, and she must, by the time she is a star, have mastered thirty or forty roles, although she may not be ready to sing all of them at a moment's notice. If she gives concerts between opera seasons she must learn many shorter songs as well, and she must always be ready to learn a part in a new opera.

We have already indicated that modern opera singers, with a few notable exceptions, are not temperamental. A display of "temperament" by a singer is usually shrewdly calculated to obtain publicity, a higher salary, or merely a better dressing room. As it interrupts the work of an opera company, it is regarded as a nuisance. It was tolerated at rehearsal only when singers were more important than the music. Nowadays only the most famous artists are ever above the rules. Toscanini's outbursts outdid those of his sopranos and tenors, and if temperament is regarded as a sign of stupidity, which it is not, conductors and singers must be considered equally stupid.

The absurdity of the belief that such people are stupid should be obvious. No stupid person could learn musical theory, acquire reasonable fluency in two or three languages in addition to his own, and commit to memory the words, notes, and cues that the average opera singer takes in his stride. During a performance, the singer must sing his own part beautifully while the orchestra and the other members of the cast are playing or singing melodies of their own, must go through at least the motions of acting, keep an eye on the conductor to follow the beat, while pretending not to do so, and not allow the size of the audience or the movements of the stagehands preparing for the next scene to distract him. Singing in opera requires not only years of training but a tremendous power of concentration.

Perhaps it is the decrease in the number of displays of temperament that leads to the lament that live singers are not as good as dead ones. There have never been many great singers at one time. There are probably more now than there ever were. If they do not stand out so much it is because they are scattered all over the world, there are more artists to share the spotlight, and critics have become more critical, often because they have a need to prove that they know more than the singers.

One teacher and coach who has watched the changes in singers for several decades says flatly that modern singers are better trained in music than their famous predecessors, are better actors, and are generally superior. Comparisons of great singers of the past with those of the present rely too much on the memory of old men who regret the passing of "the good old days." We sometimes hear the same lament about figures in sports—except in areas where meaningful records can be kept. It then becomes clear that the old runners and swimmers never approached the performances of the best present-day stars.

This does not necessarily prove that modern singers are better. But it does indicate that the lament, "There are no longer any great voices" is merely a variant of "The good old days are dead," or "Young people are not what they were in my day." There is an element of truth in all of these. Young people are different nowadays and so are opera singers, because the world in which they are living is different. The complaint that voices were no longer as great as they had been was first heard when male sopranos died out, and then it was true, for no other voices resembled theirs. But the same complaint continued to be

Left: *Maria Malibran, a singer of the nineteenth century.* Below: *Joan Sutherland, coloratura soprano, in a scene from Donizetti's* Lucia di Lammermoor, *as presented at the Paris Opéra.*

heard generation after generation, obviously coming from critics who had no idea that the future would present the world with the voices of Malibran, Melba, and Caruso, and in our own times of Birgit Nilsson, Joan Sutherland, Renata Tebaldi, Maria Callas, Boris Christoff, Mario del Monaco, Franco Corelli, and many others.

One feature of operatic life that has changed little over the centuries is backstage politics and intrigue. These still go on, as they do in every institution from government office to hospital. But performers have too much to do to spend much time on them, and a great deal of the intrigue is carried on by non-performing husbands, wives, and mothers of the stars. The performers themselves are often very helpful to each other. Gone are the days when a husband and wife, as tenor and soprano, were deadly rivals, each going into the audience to hiss when the other sang. A half century ago, Lilli Lehmann, a great Wagnerian soprano, could still carry on in the old tradition, singing the love duet from *Tristan and Isolde* with her tenor husband, and then going home to berate him for his off-pitch performance. Nowadays, such a hate duet would be impossible. Operatic husband and wife who fail to make beautiful music together usually get a divorce.

The modern opera world is so large that the day by day and year by year intimacy that once led to deadly rivalry no longer exists. It is difficult for personal hatreds to develop between people who are so often on the move. During a single opera season a soprano may sing in Buenos Aires, San Francisco, New York, London, Stockholm, and Milan. She is less concerned with the publicity some rival may receive than by the fact that in flying from Buenos Aires to San Francisco she may be changing seasons—from late spring, for example, to early winter. She may be troubled by the change in altitude between New York and Mexico City, which affects her breathing, or by the change in time zone from New York to Milan, which gives her insomnia.

As modern air travel makes the world shrink, she must be more and more concerned with protecting her voice, which undergoes enough strain as it is. A mild cold or sore throat, which the non-singer can shrug off, becomes a major catastrophe to her, for she must either cancel her performance, which is considered unforgivable, or go on stage slightly hoarse or breathless, to be told by the perceptive critics that her voice is no longer what it used to be. Just as a violinist is often overprotective of his hands, she is in danger of becoming obsessed with the need to protect her voice, and may get so tense that her voice suffers from her very preoccupation with it.

Fortunately, the human voice can take considerable abuse without permanent damage, but just as individuals differ in their resistance to colds, singers' voices differ in their resistance to strain. Some singers develop what is called "nodes," which are growths on the vocal cords. These may be removed surgically, but there is always danger of their returning unless the strain on the voice decreases.

Singers, as should be clear by now, must be highly adaptable. They must be ready to perform a number of roles under the most varied circumstances, and also must be ready to change their manner of performance of the same role from one day to the next. Even at the same opera house, on Tuesday a singer may perform with one conductor and group of singers, and on Thursday with a second group. And between an opera house in London and one in Milan, there may be a world of difference. Conductors differ in their approaches to the opera, their colleagues sing their duets differently, even the stage is differently constructed, and the audience has different customs. They may even be asked to sing the same role in English in London, in German in Vienna, and in Italian in Milan. No wonder they have small patience with the super-critic who sits back and listens for flaws in their singing—and then misses the ones that do exist, and finds some that don't.

For the few singers who reach the top ranks, the rewards are great. They have been great ever since opera became popular. Even in Handel's day, in the early eighteenth century, a famous singer could earn $25,000 a year—and in terms of modern buying power, that is equivalent to possibly $250,000. Moreover, it was practically untaxed. Enrico Caruso, in the early days of our century, earned $2,500 a performance at the Metropolitan and considerably more for concerts.

The income of singers dropped during the days of the depression in the Thirties, when a top price of $1,000 a performance was set for a few stars, while supporting singers, even in the Metropolitan Opera House, started at $60 a week. Present salaries are negotiated between each singer and management, but they probably range from a few hundred dollars a performance for secondary roles (and much less for bit parts) to possibly $2,000 a performance for top stars. It is difficult to secure accurate reports because published figures cannot be trusted. It is believed that the importance of a singer is magnified when his salary is multiplied for publication.

The salaries of singers are less than they were fifty years ago (this may be another reason for the impression in some quarters that their voices must also be inferior), but additional financial rewards can come from performances on TV, in movies, and—when the voice is going or gone—even in night clubs. Most singers, however, who are capable of singing in opera, prefer to sing there, whatever the salary.

the director 8

Some years ago, the management of the Metropolitan Opera in New York had what was hailed as a wonderful idea. The staging of many of its operas was old and out of date. Why not do them afresh, with the help of directors who had already shown their talents in the spoken drama? Opera could use new blood and new methods. Here was a chance to get both.

The directors chosen included a number of famous theatrical personalities, who were hailed with a great deal of fanfare, and who were given *carte blanche* for the operas assigned to them (or so they thought). On Broadway, a top director might receive a fee of five thousand dollars, plus two percent of the gross box office receipts until the investment in the play was recovered; then three percent, along with possibly five percent of the profits. The Metropolitan did not make public its financial arrangements with these top directors, but it was clear that the fees would be considerably lower. Apparently every one concerned thought that the result would be worth the sacrifice.

The experiment turned out to be an interesting one, but it was hardly a complete success. The staging of opera turned out to offer less room for novelty than most stage people supposed, and some of the novelties that were introduced were not well received. The directors themselves experienced considerable frustration. One exceptional director foresaw that the music would greatly affect the stage action. She therefore familiarized herself with the music on recordings, studied the libretto and its relation to the music, and before work with the singers began, spent most of the summer manipulating toy actors on the stage of a doll theatre to learn what problems she would face. With an approach of this kind, the actual direction went fairly smoothly. But the director was overwhelmed with difficulties resulting from insufficient rehearsal time and the interference of the conductor, members of the cast, and the management.

Other directors fared even less happily. When the experiment was over, the Metropolitan returned to the old custom of having its operas staged by men who had received operatic training. It still brings in an occasional theatrical director from Broadway or off-Broadway, but this is done, it seems, largely to increase the box office receipts.

One of the lessons the newcomers learned was that the director of an opera has most of the headaches of the director of a spoken play and a few special ones as well, all set to music. And he receives less glory. The director of a stage play is often revered as a genius—the single person who can make an otherwise dead play come alive. No one in this country ascribes such magical powers to the director of an opera. Nonetheless, if he lacks glory, he does not lack responsibilities. He must stage the opera so as to obtain the greatest possible comic and dramatic effects, he must move his singers and choruses about the stage in such a way as to create effective spectacles without having them get in each other's way, and he must not interfere with the music.

This is the most important feature of his work, and the most frustrating to a director accustomed to plays in which music is either absent or of minor importance. Under almost all circumstances, the music in opera takes first place and the director is subordinate to the composer, whether the latter is living or dead. He is therefore not free to invent action or stage business as he would in a spoken play. The composer has built a framework within which the singers must work. If the stage directions read, "A man enters," and three measures later the man gives vent to his emotions in song, the entrance must be complete in those three measures.

Duels, fights, battles, shipwrecks, and all other stage events must take place within a definite number of beats. Action may have to be compressed or extended, as the composer has ruled. A dramatic murder may take five seconds to commit, although the murdered man may take half an hour to die. The director must think of bits of action for the dying man to perform while the audience listens to him.

The conductor, as executor of the composer's will, may give the stage action a bit more leeway by taking the music at a slower pace, or he may compress things even more by going at a rapid clip. In any case, the director does not create his own tempo, but has it given to him. Only if the music stops altogether, as may happen in a comic opera, is the director fairly free to invent stage business at his own tempo.

Other factors also complicate the life of the opera director. On the speaking stage he is usually called on to direct a new play or, occasionally, the revival of a classic by someone like Shakespeare, Ibsen, or O'Neill. But the opera director rarely has the chance to work on a new opera. Most of the time he puts on operas that have been performed thousands of times all over the world or, with less popular operas, several hundred times. He may venture on a new interpretation, but as a rule the public likes to see old favorites done in the same old way, the singers like to sing the roles as they have learned them, and there is always the awareness that the conductor is boss. If there are to be any new interpretations, they will be *his* interpretations. In opera, stage direction is the tail, and it rarely succeeds in wagging the dog.

The shortness of rehearsal time limits everyone concerned with an opera. Therefore, any really difficult stage action is out of the question. In one memorable performance of *La Gioconda,* the unfortunate tenor had his foot caught in a fish net, and possibly as a result, became confused and lost his place in his big aria. In this same performance, the soprano found herself trapped in a boat, and had to struggle so furiously to get out that one critic said the next day that she was "in strident voice."

She was probably just yelling in frustration, and she was justified. Such difficulties usually arise from the lack of stage rehearsals. A composer may ask the performers to sing while climbing a tree or fighting a duel, and although such feats are by no means impossible, they require careful rehearsal. The breathing of the singer must be coordinated with the action, and mistakes are sure to happen at first. With rehearsal time limited, the tendency is to fall back on the easiest sort of behavior, which consists of singing while standing still in one spot. Once a long aria or duet begins, therefore, the simplest way out of the director's difficulties is to have hero and heroine meet in the center of the stage, face the audience instead of each other, and burst into song. The director may disdain so primitive an approach, but more complicated action will cause trouble.

The stage director begins with a reading of the play, and after the actors have acquired some familiarity with it, he analyzes and discusses the characters and their behavior. There is no time for this in most operas, and unfortunately, most of the cast will feel that there is no need for it. They have played the parts before. Why waste time going over what they already know?

Enrico Caruso, the tenor whose fame is almost legendary, is saved from the noose by Emmy Destinn, a noted soprano of the period, in the final act of The Girl of the Golden West *by Puccini. No stage director today would stage a scene this way.*

This attitude is undoubtedly wrong. In the last few years, operatic productions at the Komische Oper in Berlin have been among the best in the world. Here the director, Walter Felsenstein, has been in a very fortunate position, for he has been general manager of the opera house as well, and has escaped the usual fate of being subordinate to the conductor. The quality of his productions has been remarkable because circumstances permitted both a thorough study of each opera and adequate time for rehearsal. Rehearsals might take months, but no opera was presented until it was ready. When invited to do Mozart's *Don Giovanni* at a famous opera house, Felsenstein demanded a year and a half for rehearsals. The demand was not granted, and the invitation was not accepted.

Contrast this with what happens in the usual opera house, where every experienced singer thinks he knows all about *Don Giovanni,* and rehearsals serve only to give the performers some feeling of familiarity with the particular sets and costumes and possibly with the acoustics of the opera house.

Among the other difficulties of the stage director are the need for training either two casts of singers for each opera, or a number of substitutes. As singers differ in stage presence and acting ability, the director must choose between two unpalatable alternatives: either to direct each cast differently, and thus increase the work he must do, or else direct both in the same

Act III of Tales of Hoffmann *by Offenbach, as performed at the Komische Oper in Berlin. The director, Felsenstein, rehearses each production for many months.*

way, and have some of the singers act in ways that do not suit them.

In opera as in a spoken play, the prime duty of the director is to devise the stage action. He must think of something for every character to do, insofar as the action is not obviously determined by the requirements of the dialogue, the stage directions, or a ballet. A soprano preparing to do her big aria cannot be left simply standing in the center of the stage. Attention must be directed to her at the proper time, and in addition she must be given something to do while waiting, so that she may forget her voice for a few moments and be reasonably relaxed.

When a well-known opera is being performed, it is fairly easy to figure out how much of the credit or blame for a performance should go to the director, and how much to the performers. Usually, any new forms of action can be safely credited to the director, including the new facial expressions of a singer who has played an old role in a new way.

Facial expression is only one of the special difficulties that beset the opera director. Singing is best done with a mouth opened wide, as if for a difficult tooth extraction. This hardly permits the proper expression of delicate emotions since, among other things, it compresses the eyes to slits. Therefore, a singer expressing love, for example, must do so with her voice, her arms, and her body, but not with her face. It is only when she is listening to some one else's expression of love that her face can become properly rapturous.

But then, a mild expression of rapture is not enough, for opera houses are usually so large that most of the audience is quite a distance from the stage, and facial expressions as well as gestures must be much more exaggerated than they are on the usual theatre stage. The tenth-row spectator may complain that a singer is violently overacting, while to a viewer in the remotest part of the balcony her performance may seem entirely realistic. The director must keep the entire audience in mind, and compromise accordingly.

Directing an opera requires a great amount of detailed work because of the large size of many of the casts and the huge stage that must sometimes be covered. The director must also stage crowd scenes, with masses of people grouped for singing, or involved in mock battles. These are rare in modern spoken drama because they cost too much, but they are commonplace in opera.

Animals present still other problems. Producers early learned the value of even the tamest of beasts in creating spectacular effects. The menagerie that *Berenice* used back in 1680 was used again by Verdi two centuries later in *Aïda,* with camels and more elephants substituted for deer and bears.

In the days of *Berenice,* the direction of an unwieldy human and animal cast usually fell to the conductor. No high degree of skill was expected in the staging, and it was enough that the performers were seen at more or less the right places at the right time for, among other difficulties, the problem of lighting was a formidable one. Dozens of torches were prepared, lit especially for the spectacular scenes, and distributed to the animal attendants. The scene became a picture of men and beasts, marching around the stage in a flickering pattern of light and shadow that thrilled the spectators, and if any of the performers was not exactly on cue, no one knew or cared.

With the advent first of gas and later of electric lighting, the stage became a better lit place as well as a safer one, and it was easy to see when anything went wrong. The task of the director became more exacting.

Toward the end of the nineteenth century, Richard Wagner, with his emphasis on the unity of all aspects of music drama, had paid attention to the problem of staging. Not until half a century later, however, did stage direction finally become a separate province, under the general supervision of the conductor, although no longer his direct responsibility.

The conductor had to relinquish his grasp simply because he had so many other things to do, and directing took a man's full time. The director has, with rare exceptions, therefore, acted as assistant to the conductor, and as his duties have grown, he too has acquired assistants—young directors who supervise the movements of the chorus, the supers, or other special groups in a large cast, such as the stagehands involved in producing special stage effects, or the goats, geese, and children that appear in some operas.

What happened in opera parallels to some extent what happened with spoken plays. Here the star actor once formed his own troupe, and the actor-manager took over any direction that seemed to be required. In general his tendency was to build up his own part and neglect the rest of the play. The composer-conductor, as director, similarly was likely not only to emphasize the prime importance of the music, which was proper, but also to neglect the staging. Only when direction was handed over to a specialist did it receive its due.

Unlike the director of spoken plays, the director of the opera can usually count on no long runs, no great royalties. He usually works on a salary as an employee of the opera company or, when brought in to direct a single opera, on a flat fee plus royalty basis. In some small opera houses, as in Italy, there may be no director, the function being taken over by the general manager of the opera, or handed back to the conductor.

As assistant to a number of conductors, the director faces a recurrent difficulty: an opera never remains the same. Very few operas are performed uncut, and in every opera house, the cuts are different. Also, every conductor conducts differently. It is ironic that Wagner, who so emphasized the unity of music and words, wrote some of the longest music dramas in the repertory, and is therefore most frequently cut, so that his precious unity is destroyed. The director who comes to a new opera house is therefore uncertain, until he has consulted with the conductor or seen a new version of the score, exactly what scenes will be left in, and how much they will be curtailed. The variety possible in the cutting complicates his task enormously. By eliminating one section or another, or by eliminating only certain spoken or musical phrases, the conductor can throw an entirely new light on an opera, can emphasize one feature at the expense of another, and can thus demand an entirely new directional approach.

This highlights one of the director's greatest problems: his point of view as an artist. Like the director of a spoken play, he must decide what the opera means to him, emotionally and intellectually, and then he must convince the conductor that his interpretation offers great dramatic and musical possibilities, and is consistent with the conductor's own approach. He must choose between the easy, traditional way of doing an opera, and a new interpretation which may be artistically superior, but will certainly meet with objection from some one in a supervisory position, from singers, and from much of the audience as well. It is so much safer to do things in the same old way that few professional opera directors succumb to the temptation to be original.

If the director of opera has his difficulties, he also has advantages over the director of spoken drama. He has no casting problems. The performers are chosen chiefly for their ability to sing, and although his advice may be sought, the final responsibility is not his. There is no difficulty about remembering lines.

These are part of the music, to be sung, not spoken, and they are the responsibility of the conductor. Best of all, there are none of the headaches involved in rewriting. A play is often changed from rehearsal to rehearsal, depending on the response of the audience that sees it tried out, and the director must, of course, change the staging accordingly.

Clearly, the director's task is an exacting one. He must be a good musician, he must know Italian, French, and German—for these are the chief languages of opera—and he must have a good acquaintance with the standard operas. If he is foreign-born, and working with an American company, he had better know English as well, or he will be forced to work with interpreters.

He must have a background of work with small and large opera companies, so that he is familiar with the endless problems that crop up—from practical questions of cost to subtleties of artistic interpretation.

Perhaps it is just as well that he is never regarded as a miracle worker, as is the director of spoken plays. In the opera, miracles are not performed without money, and the director on a budget is restricted to purely human achievements. It is enough that he so often does a good job.

the choreographer 9

When Richard Wagner's *Tannhaüser* was first performed at Dresden, in 1845, it was well received, but Dresden was a minor center of opera compared to Paris, and an opera could not be considered completely successful until it had been performed to critical acclaim in the French capital. The Paris performance took place in 1866. Knowing the fondness of the Parisians for ballet, Wagner had provided one but, as if grudging the need to do so, he had put it at the beginning of the opera, so that it would be out of the way before the serious business of the evening began.

To the aristocratic members of the "Jockey Club," whose verdict could mean success or failure for an opera, this was not playing the game. A ballet that latecomers would miss—and important people were never on time—was no ballet at all. When the first act ended, and the second act went its melodious way, without signs of a *real* ballet, members of Parisian high society began to boo and hiss, and the performance ended in a riot.

Ever since Wagner's time, the ballet has remained a sore spot in many operas. Almost a century after the booing of *Tannhaüser,* a Metropolitan Opera audience followed the great tradition by booing a ballet in Gluck's *Alceste.* Booing is evidence of a passionate dislike which is rare among American opera audiences, and the choreographer, the dance critics, and the management were all greatly upset.

It is possible that Gluck himself, if he could have been revived to attend the performance, would have booed also, for the dance composed to his music was like no ballet he had ever seen. This does not mean that it was a bad one. But it was not the kind of dancing Gluck had in mind, or the kind to which opera audiences were accustomed. It was too modern, too much involved with the unconscious psychology of its characters, too far removed from the classical tradition of ballet. It might have been properly appreciated by a modern ballet audience. It was thrown away on an average audience of modern American opera-lovers.

These same American opera-lovers do appreciate ballets that accord with their sense of what is right. They will applaud more conventional ballets in *Aïda,* or in Gluck's *Alceste,* for that matter, as well as in the other two dozen operas that are put on in the course of a season. What they like, however, the choreographer is likely to disparage as "old stuff." And very often it is.

For this and other reasons, the choreographer for opera is likely to be unhappy. Once the librettist and composers have done their work, he is one of the few people connected with an opera who can be said to create, for conductor and singers are, after all, performers and interpreters, while the creative activity of the director is limited by the restrictions of the libretto and score. The choreographer must accomplish his creation, however, with a work that is often a hundred or more years old. As with the operas of Gluck, the style of the music and the nature of the story usually demand dances to correspond. The modern choreographer often ends up, therefore, by contriving dances that offer nothing original, which he does not regard

Anthony Tudor, left, rehearsing a group of Metropolitan Opera dancers in the ballet studio.

as creations at all. He hopes the opera management and the audience will like them, but he doesn't.

Thus, like the conductor and director, he tends to play it safe, to do things in the traditional way, to upset no one by the intrusion of novelty. And indeed, unless there is a new approach by all the artists involved, novelty is out of place. A production should have a unity of approach, or else it becomes confusing.

In this country, the choreographer and ballet director (usually the same person) for opera has little to do in the final production. In *Aïda* there may be fifteen minutes of dancing; in most operas the dancing takes only five or ten minutes. For these few minutes of performance each evening, the corps de ballet works for five or six hours a day. In this country there is no second cast for the minor parts in an opera, or for the members of the ballet. Therefore, the dancers dance night after night, rehearse and practice day after day, and by the end of a five-month season are near exhaustion. Never has so much work gone into producing so little.

Some of the choreographer's difficulty arises from the fact that the chief effects of an opera are created for the ear, while his are created for the eye. Confirmed opera-goers attend to see and hear favorite singers, or to listen to the music, not primarily to see the ballet. Those who love ballet consider it a waste of time and money to attend a performance in which there is so little dancing. Again the choreographer is reminded that he is creating for an audience that is not his own.

In most European countries the situation is quite different. In France and England the first operas had to compete with the ballet and the masque— one entirely a dance form and the other containing many dances. To attract a dance audience, the opera had to offer dances of its own, and the tradition has not only been maintained in France and England but has spread to the countries near by. The ballet therefore is more important in European opera, and choreographers there are more highly appreciated. Ballet scenes are not cut or shortened as they sometimes are in this country, and may in fact be extended by repetition or by addition of other music by the same composer.

In Europe also there may be fewer problems in fitting the style of the ballet to that of the opera. Some of the European

Act II of Die Götterdämmerung *by Wagner, as performed at the Bayreuth Festival. Realistic scenery is discarded in favor of the stark basic set, which combines with lighting effects to create a highly stylized, imaginative setting for the* Ring *operas.*

ballet companies, such as the Danish or the Soviet, have clung to traditional styles of dancing and of operatic production, and little conflict exists between the two. In countries like Germany, where modern dance has been popular, many of the operas too are performed in more stylized versions; that is, unrealistically, with over-simplified scenery and greater reliance than usual on lighting effects. Such an approach offers much greater opportunity to a modern choreographer.

In all countries, however, whether highly appreciated or not, the choreographer does face the problems that arise as a result of working with so many people who are not directly concerned with the dance. The conductor is interested chiefly in musical values; the director wishes to subordinate the dancing to the general stage action; the scene designer may have ideas for scenery that severely limits the dancing space. As is natural, when such conflicts occur, the one who gets his way is usually the one with the most authority and prestige. In this free-for-all, the choreographer usually comes out with a minor share of the spoils.

Despite all these troubles, the choreographer does add to the opera-goers' enjoyment. If he didn't, he and his dancers would be eliminated. Sometimes his dances are intended to be merely a break in the main action of the opera, a diversion, or "divertissement" to use the old French term. At other times, the dancing is part of the action itself. It may be a spectacle, as in *Aïda,* or an expression of the emotions of the character, as in *Salome.* Its value to the production as a whole is much greater when it helps to tell the story of the opera.

The more the dancing is integrated into the production, however, the less freedom the choreographer has to create as he pleases. All in all, no matter what pleasure he gives to the audience, the choreographer himself rarely has reason to dance for joy.

the designer 10

THE MAN OR WOMAN who designs for the opera stage has the same responsibilities as those of the designer for any stage. He must create sets that form a suitable background for the action and are, at the same time, worth looking at for themselves. If he creates the costumes, and in many opera houses he usually does, they must faithfully depict the period of the opera and be extravagantly luxurious or ragged, according to the demands of the opera. If realism is his aim, his interior settings must give the illusion of an inn, a marble palace, or a ballroom, while his outdoor scenes must trick the eyes so that they see a genuine pyramid or cathedral.

Because most operas in the repertory are from half a century to two centuries old, and the style of the music and libretto fit the time in which they were written, the style of the scenery must be suited to it as well. An occasional old opera is played in a more modern style, just as a few of Shakespeare's dramas have been staged in modern dress, but the difficulties of doing this are greater in opera than in Shakespeare. *Hamlet* and *Julius Caesar* were written so long ago that their language seems archaic, and therefore lofty and poetic. The words of most operas seem merely old-fashioned, especially in translation.

It is true that special circumstances permit the adaptation

of a modern approach to some old operas. Such works of Gluck as *Orpheus and Eurydice* and *Alceste,* because of their classic severity, can be staged in more abstract form than *Tosca* or *Aïda.* And the settings of some of Wagner's music dramas, because they are founded on myth and legend, can be effectively stylized, that is, greatly simplified. As mentioned previously, numerous experiments in staging and lighting have been made at the special theatre built for his works at Bayreuth, Germany (see picture, page 133). But in general, the nature of grand opera, as well as the traditions of singers and conductors, have limited the freedom to experiment in stage design.

These limitations are only slowly being removed. The experiments at Bayreuth and in a few other places would not be so tempting to managers of opera if they were not reinforced by an even greater temptation—the desire to cut costs. Modern stage settings are usually stylized, impressionistic rather than realistic, with emphasis on a few elements of the stage picture at the expense of others, and on the use of symbols instead of real things. The stage contains fewer props, leaving more room for singers and dancers—but very often leaving a great deal of empty and embarrassing space when mere space is not wanted.

The effect of emptiness can be dissipated by proper lighting. Lighting is a much more important feature in modern staging than it was on the traditional stage, where its function was usually to keep singers and impressive sets visible to the audience. Now it is used to exaggerate some things and minimize others, to create effects by means of patterns of light and shade. It requires considerable imagination, and is sometimes so complicated that its creation is not attempted by the designer of the sets, but is taken over by another specialist, just as the costume designs may be.

Modern spoken plays achieve speed and greater continuity by

shifting the action from one corner of a stage to another, lighting up the particular area where the action is going on and leaving the others in darkness or dim light. This technique is rarely, if ever, used in professional opera in this country. The whole stage is ordinarily used, or at least the part of it in front of the curtain is used, while the part behind the curtain is undergoing a change of scenery. If the shifting of sets takes too long, the pace can be maintained and the mood left unbroken by appropriate orchestral transitions.

There is another reason why the nature of opera does not usually favor abstract or oversimplified settings. The inevitable sketchiness of the libretto must be overcome by other elements of the production. Shakespeare could get along with a minimum of scenery by painting word pictures, and a modern playwright can use the shock value of his dialogue to make the setting unimportant, but the composer of an opera faces a different problem. His music evokes emotion, but ordinarily not visual patterns, so that lavish scenery is almost a necessity. (Wagner was a striking exception, with his musical descriptions of forest and flame, the ride of the Valkyries, and so on.) Neither the music alone nor the combination of music and words creates a convincing picture of ancient Babylon in *Nabucco,* or of Egypt in *Aïda.*

In order to create the proper visual environment, therefore, a good scenic designer must be at least an excellent artist and a skilled architect, if not an expert at lighting and costume design as well. In addition, like every one else with a creative job in an operatic production, ideally, he should know music in general and, in particular, he should know the opera for which he is designing. This requirement is not easy to meet, for painters, sculptors, and architects usually have visual imaginations and are not well trained to imagine sounds. Many of them,

An early producton of Carmen *by Bizet. Contrast this old-fashioned set for Act II with the photograph below of a modern set for the same act as produced recently at the Paris Opéra.*

in fact, are completely ignorant of music. If they are, the production will probably suffer. An artist cannot design the most effective set for an opera, spoken play, or ballet unless he first goes through the entire production in his imagination, planning the scenery so that it is adapted to the action. As the music is an inseparable part of operatic staging, the artist who has no ear for it will imagine the action incorrectly, and his settings will reflect his mistaken concepts.

The need to cut costs has become important in the present-day theatre for both spoken plays and opera. The producer David Belasco was famous half a century ago for the naturalism of his settings, that were complete to the last authentic detail of farmhouse or cafeteria. It was his boast that he spared no expense. Nowadays, the producer spares every possible expense, presenting his plays on an almost empty stage, putting on one-set plays, or having readings before a curtain. He is now using the curtain backdrops and the simplified settings that were once the hallmark of the amateur theatre.

Opera is one of the last strongholds of the expensive set. The tradition of lavish opera sets dates from the end of the seventeenth century, when members of the Galli da Bibiena family established the pattern. This family of artists took its name from Giovanni Maria Galli, who was born in the small town of Bibbiena, near Florence. For a hundred years after 1690, he and his descendants created magnificent sets not only for operas, but also for the weddings and funerals of most of the European courts. In Verona, Bologna, Mantua, Naples, Rome, Barcelona, Vienna, Munich, Prague, Dresden, Bayreuth, London, Stockholm, and St. Petersburg, among other places, members of the family built opera houses, created indoor and outdoor sets, and sent kings and nobles to their graves in pomp. One of their most spectacular accomplishments was for *Alcina,* a ballet opera (not Handel's), when they floated giant sets on a pond in a Viennese garden.

It is a melancholy comment on the impermanence of their work that we know of it chiefly from drawings. The Royal Theatre in Mantua burned in 1781, the Dresden Opera House in 1849. Most of their other constructions were destroyed by the end of World War II, and of all their works only the auditorium of the old court theatre at Bayreuth still exists. But their designs helped to establish the supremacy of the proscenium stage over all the other stages, and had a long-lasting effect on the theatre.

The opera stage is plentifully supplied with trap doors for the entrance and exit of angels, devils, and other supernatural characters and, because a theatre may be the permanent home of many operas, it may have such features as a revolving stage or a stage that can be raised or lowered. The possibilities in some houses occasionally become overpoweringly tempting to the designer who dreams of departing from the traditional approach. Whenever his ideas will cut costs, the manager may be on his side. But the opera itself may be against him.

For instance, theatre-in-the-round—a play acted on a stage surrounded by an audience—is now a fairly well-accepted form of theatre. It permits the use of buildings not originally constructed as theatres, and brings the audience closer to the play. Opera-in-the-round, however, would have special difficulties. One of the most obvious is the requirement that orchestra and singers keep their eyes on the conductor, which means that the conductor must be in front of the stage. Theatre-in-the-round has no "front of the stage."

Nevertheless, the round stage has been used for the successful production of musical comedy, and it has been suggested for serious opera as well, on the ground that it would increase the size of the audience and thus help to meet production costs more

A stage design by V. Colosanti for Verdi's Otello, *as presented by Maggio Musicale Fiorentino, in Florence, Italy.*

quickly. Where greater intimacy between singers and audience is desired, as in a folk opera, there might be artistic advantages as well. Wagner's music dramas, however, among many other serious operas, require not greater intimacy, but a feeling of remoteness, and here opera-in-the-round would mean a loss of artistic quality.

The designer of scenery and of costumes must consider what he can contribute to the opera as a whole, but very often his most important role is to enhance the effect of the opening curtain and of one or two important scenes in each act. Therefore, he is likely to start by imagining what he will show the audience for the very first scene of the opera. Sometimes on opening night he is rewarded by a gasp of surprise and delight and a round of applause that show he has triumphed.

But the conductor, the director, and the singers are not so easily satisfied. The designer's sets must do more than dazzle at first sight. They must allow the singers to carry out the action that composer, librettist, and director have devised for them.

In the final act of *Boris Godunov,* for instance, Boris, the dying Czar of Russia, sings of his feelings at the approach of death, and then, in an agony of fear, rolls down a flight of steps from his throne. The designer, with his knowledge of perspective, can contribute to the tremendous effect of this scene by making the steps seem higher than they are, but, at the same time, must construct them so that the singer can roll down them without injuring himself.

While devoting special attention to such climatic scenes, the designer must not neglect the rest of the opera. During the least interesting passages, as in recitative, when the characters do not sing but simply narrate what is happening, audiences often become restless, and their eyes are likely to stray. If the designer knows his business, they will have something interesting to stray to.

The designer must plan his sets in outline and be sure of the approval of his colleagues before going ahead with them. He makes his first rough sketches in black and white, with notes about color and lighting, and discusses them with conductor, director, choreographer, and manager. The first three are interested in the artistic effect of the sets, but must also consider whether the cast will find them useful and not too confusing. If there are to be a hundred people in a scene, the director must be sure they will be able to move around freely. The choreographer, too, will demand enough room for the dancers.

The conductor may caution against the use of too many levels,

Act II of The Masked Ball *by Verdi at La Scala Opera House. This stunning set serves to highlight the action.*

for although many operas make use of staircases or of balconies and platforms of different heights, slight changes in level are easily overlooked by the cast, and are more disconcerting than in a spoken play. A singer must keep his eye on the conductor to get the beat, and although he is not likely to bump into a piece of furniture or a staircase unless he is extremely near-sighted, he is always in danger of tripping over a single step. The director and the manager as well examine the settings carefully for such booby traps. When a fishnet or a boat trips a singer, they share the blame with the designer.

The costumes must be rich when richness is called for, and they must be comfortable. A tenor or soprano has enough difficulty sustaining a high note without having a tight collar to make it more difficult.

The manager is also interested in the general artistic quality of the production, but, as a rule, he is willing to leave this to the conductor and director. After all, he selected them. His main concern is cost. The shadow of the budget hangs over every production, and many a set that disappoints an audience is the unhappy result of compromise between the designer's original idea and his attempt to meet the manager's demand that he carry it out cheaply.

Once the rough sketches and ideas have been approved or amended, the designer makes more detailed sketches in watercolor. If these are approved, he then supervises the actual creation of the sets. He likes to do the lighting too if he has time, for the lighting is part of his visualization of the scenic background of the opera. So too are the costumes, but lack of time, and more rarely, of skill, may force a division of labor between scene designer and costume designer.

We have indicated that the designer must be an artist; it should now be clear that he must also be an extremely practical man, aware of the requirements of every element of the production. As an artist, he must be acquainted with the art and architecture of different historical periods and be a faithful patron of museums. As a practical man, he must know something about lighting and electricity and have an intimate acquaintance with paints and materials, which are changing from year to year. He must construct his sets so that they are easily shifted and at the same time are sturdy enough to be used year after year. From time to time he may have to arrange for the retouching of old sets, possibly with minor alterations in design that will deceive an audience into thinking it is seeing something new, without subjecting the company to the actual expense of new sets. Nothing can be more practical than that.

A little of what he must know is taught in schools of art and drama, but by far the greater portion of his ability comes from natural talent and from experience. Experience with sets on television and spoken drama is useful, but before he can become a full-fledged designer for the operatic stage, he must work in opera itself. He may start as assistant to anyone who works backstage, from manager to director. This will help him to learn in general how to deal with the situations a stage designer faces. The opportunity to go on to a more important position then depends on recognition of his talent by people in authority—and on luck. He needs as much luck as talent if he hopes to displace an established designer and survive the competition of the dozen other young designers looking for the same job.

opera without glamour 11

THE MEN AND WOMEN who are part of opera for the artistic satisfaction it affords are far outnumbered by those to whom opera is chiefly a way to earn a living, and whose jobs are without glamour. These people have no hopes and fears about press notices and no illusions about being remembered for their triumphs. They may perform highly skilled duties without which the opera could not go on, but they can be replaced by equally skilled persons, without changing the character of the performance.

Perhaps first place among these dispensable indispensables belongs to the orchestral musicians. Everyone of them has been trained to be an artist, and many of them are artists when they perform individually. But their status as artists is doubtful when they perform in an opera orchestra. It is the conductor who decides on the interpretation of the music, who tells them to play loudly or softly, and it is the requirements of the opera as a whole which usually force them to become mere accompanists to the singers. Their work continues to require a high degree of musical skill but, like stagehands and box office men, they regard it as a job and not as art. Only occasionally, in a solo passage here and there, do they have occasion to become artists again.

On the other hand, the members of the stage crew are trained to be craftsmen and remain craftsmen at all times. Among them are carpenters, electricians, prop men—who handle the numerous objects seen on stage during a production—and stage hands—who shift scenery. In addition, the backstage area is home to the make-up artists and to the men and women who create the scenery under the supervision of the designer, and to the wardrobe department.

The handling of scenery and costumes is much more compli-

The prop room at the Paris Opéra. Despite the jumble any piece that is needed can be quickly identified.

This part of the electric board at the Metropolitan controls the electric pipes on which back drops are raised and lowered.

cated in opera than in an ordinary spoken play. To some extent, as was brought out in the previous chapter, this is because opera still demands more scenery than is customary in modern plays. But, in addition, an opera company like the Metropolitan is also a repertory company, putting on twenty-five works a season with an average of half a dozen performances each. It has in reserve dozens of operas that are brought out every few years. The backstage area is not large enough for the storage of sets for so many operas, and it has been necessary each day, and sometimes twice a day, to move sets from warehouse to stage and back again. While waiting to be moved, sets are frequently left outside the building during rain and snow. As a result, they must be touched up and repaired from time to time, until finally they look so definitely decrepit that they are thrown away and replaced entirely. The problem is then passed on to management.

Many operas have tremendous casts, with as many as several hundred supers and chorus members. (Supers have walk-on, nonsinging parts, and are hired when needed—not for the season.) All of these must be in costume. Thousands of costumes are,

Making up for a performance of Aïda *at the San Francisco Opera.*

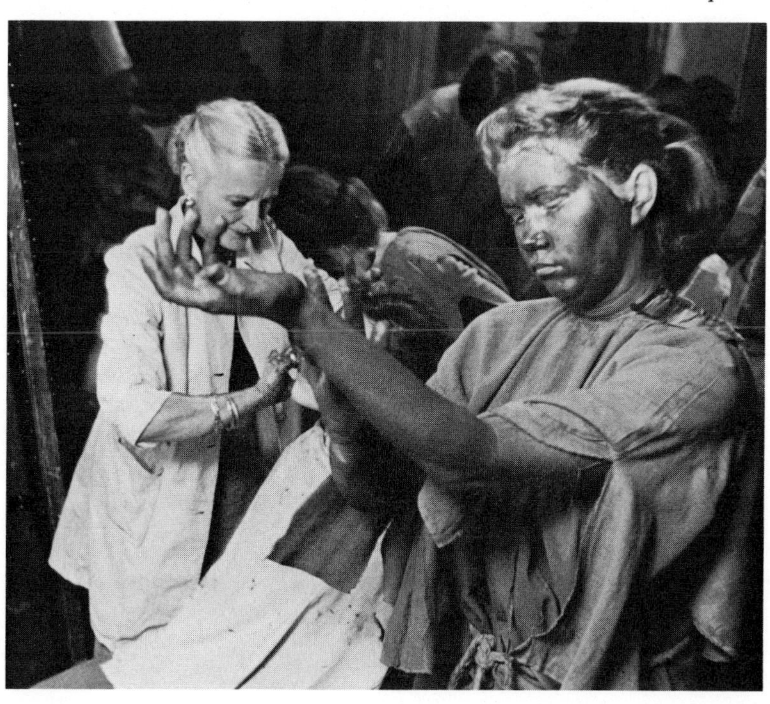

therefore, needed during the year, and all must be arranged so that they can be found and identified without loss of time. They must also be kept clean and in repair. Americans have been growing larger and taller over the years, and costumes have constantly to be altered for them. Damaged costumes have to be replaced. These are problems of the wardrobe and dressmaking departments and, obviously, they are kept busy.

Most attention is paid to the costumes of the star singers, and these present special problems. When a production is newly designed, costumes are made for the entire cast, including the principals, who are expected to wear costumes that harmonize with the rest of the production. Difficulty may arise if an old-fashioned, padded soprano replaces a modern streamlined one, but the wardrobe department can usually make suitable alterations. In productions that have not been redesigned for many years, however, some of the costumes seem ridiculous, and it has long been the custom to permit visiting stars to bring their own. The visitor's costume may then clash disastrously with some elements of the rest of the production, and seem even more ridiculous. For this reason, the practice of importing costumes, though traditional, is not encouraged.

There are, of course, numerous ushers, janitors, engineers, and box office men whose work is essential but requires no discussion.

The publicity department, however, does deserve some comment. As in every other field where publicity is needed, it is the function of a publicity man to put a good face on everything that happens, and occasionally to make a virtue of unpleasant necessities. If the manager cannot get the soprano he wants, the soprano he gets must be hailed as the best of her kind.

All this is like the job of any theatrical publicity department. There is, nonetheless, a difference. The publicity for a play or movie is aimed chiefly at keeping all the seats of a theatre filled, as each empty seat means either a decrease in profits or an actual loss. The publicity of the Metropolitan is what is called "institutional," concerned more with opera in general and with the producing organization than with individual operas or individual artists. Performances of *Aïda* or *Don Giovanni* are fairly sure to fill the house under any circumstances, and an empty seat more or less means little to a non-profit organization that usually sells out about ninety-five percent of the available tickets.

It is the future that worries the publicity department of an opera more than the present. Because the entire entertainment field has changed so radically in the past twenty years and is likely to change even more, publicity must be aimed at keeping the opera alive for many years to come, and not merely during the current season.

In other words, an opera audience must be built and held not only for the performance of a particular evening, but for seasons five, ten, and twenty years ahead. This problem is a formidable one, and it is faced by every opera company in the United States and Canada, from the Metropolitan down to the amateur groups in small cities.

It cannot be handled by a publicity department alone, which is why such organizations as the Metropolitan Opera Guild and the National Council of the Metropolitan Opera Association have been formed. The purpose of the former is to advance the interests of opera among the general public by building audiences and securing financial support, while the function of the latter is to exchange information among groups that produce opera, and to help them with problems of production and fund-raising. It gives advice on the obtaining of costumes, props, and suitable translations. Both groups cooperate with each other and with the publicity department of the Metropolitan Opera.

All the different ways of creating interest in opera are directed to the same end. A high school student who has attended a first-class performance of opera on a student ticket will not only have a greater interest in attending opera in future but will also be more interested in taking part in amateur opera groups. And, conversely, the participants in amateur companies throughout the country are among those most interested in attending professional performances.

In encouraging this kind of activity, the publicity department plays a minor role. The initiative is in the hands of the Opera Guild and the National Council.

Among the other groups in the opera company are the wigmakers, and the call department, which notifies the different people who take part in a performance. Because the same performance does not take place night after night, it is easy for some of the lesser members of a cast to lose track of their schedule. The call department reminds them. There is a librarian to take care of the precious scores of the numerous operas, with all the special cuts and arrangements used in the past. There is also a baggage crew which is needed when the opera gives its performances on the road.

Among the more numerous non-artists are the "supers"—the men and women who carry spears, march in processions, and take part in crowd scenes when members of chorus and ballet are not enough to fill the stage or are otherwise engaged. In the past they were chosen rather haphazardly, and sometimes ruined performances by arriving late. Now they are generally chosen from ballet or theatre students on the basis of appearance and stage presence. They usually have but a few moments on stage, but during those few moments they must wear their costumes well and be part of the opera, marching sedately or rioting wildly as the script demands. Their salary has risen from twenty-five

How helmets and swords are stored by the Metropolitan Opera wardrobe department.

cents a performance in 1880 to two dollars for each performance or rehearsal now.

Finally, there is a group that was once an unofficial part of every large opera organization and is now rarely found—the claque. This consisted of men and women whose business it was to applaud. They were paid by individual singers for each performance, starting the handclapping after an aria, and going on to unrestrained cries of "Bravo!" if the enthusiasm of the audience appeared to warrant it—and if they had been paid enough. They both led and stimulated the applause, keeping it going by apparently spontaneous bursts of new enthusiasm whenever it showed signs of dying down. As inveterate opera-goers, they knew exactly when to begin and how to build toward a climax, and the satisfaction they gave the singer was more soothing to his ego than a visit to a psychoanalyst. Less knowledgable members of the audience, afraid of applauding at the wrong time, were often grateful too. Sometimes they were paid to hiss a rival in addition to cheering their patron of the evening, and on occasion there would be a clash between rival claques, first one cheering and the other hissing, and then the two groups changing roles as the different singers appeared.

At the Metropolitan and at most other leading operas, the claque, which is supposed to have been first formed in Roman times two thousand years ago, no longer exists. At most, a singer may distribute free tickets to friends in exchange for applause. Although the claque may still linger on in a few small Italian opera houses where traditions change slowly, it is on its way out as far as opera is concerned. But there is a new version of the claque that can be found on television in the form of "canned" applause. In its older form, however, the claque was more satisfying to the performer's ego.

Before any egos can be satisfied, much hard work lies ahead for all the performers. We have noted that calls for the rehearsal of *Aïda* go out in September. Let us see what happens at these exhausting and sometimes painful rehearsal sessions.

rehearsal 12

As rehearsals begin, the orchestra members assemble with the conductor. The chorus gathers elsewhere under the leadership of an assistant conductor who has been appointed chorus master for the season, and the leading singers and their alternates embark on sessions with other assistants. The director, the conductor, and the assistant conductors must divide their attention among soloists, chorus, and orchestra. Every session must therefore be properly scheduled so that conductor or director will not be expected to be in two places at once.

The rehearsal schedule is a circus which at times has many more than three rings. The orchestra has only the morning to devote to *Aïda.* In the afternoon it will be reading another operatic score with a different conductor, and in this manner it will go on day after day, reviewing different operas morning and afternoon, and returning to *Aïda* for a total of possibly four to six rehearsals during the season.

At its first rehearsal, the chorus is greeted by the chorus master, who arranges it in groups according to voice—sopranos in one section, altos, tenors, and basses in others. The chorus has a good deal of singing to do in *Aïda,* and, in addition, being composed of priests, priestesses, soldiers, and ordinary Egyptians, takes part in the operatic action as the orchestra does not. It

A Metropolitan artists' and chorus rehearsal in a studio.

must wear Egyptian costumes and learn to move about the stage without becoming an unruly mob and without getting in the way of the soloists.

The chorus master will concentrate on those sections of the music which are most important and offer the greatest difficulty. He may start, for instance, with the temple scene at the end of Act I, where the entire company, from soloists to ballet, is performing. The women's chorus is backstage, heard but not seen. The Egyptians are praying and offering sacrifices to the gods for victory in the war against the Ethiopians, and Rhadames, the Egyptian general who is the hero of the opera, receives the consecration of the priests.

The music is first read by the chorus members, all musical entrances being carefully noted, and the scene is repeated a number of times to correct errors and achieve greater musical and verbal clarity. The conductor will stop and start the singers again and again, until he is satisfied that they not only know the notes but are following all his signals for crescendos, diminuendos, and so on. Among professional musicians the ability to sing the notes is taken for granted. It is the ability to carry out the musical ideas of the composer and conductor that distinguishes the good professional from the mediocre one, and it is the need to have all the singers work as a team that requires extended rehearsal.

When he is satisfied that the scene is reasonably under control, the chorus master will turn to another part of the score, perhaps the triumphal return of the army, which concludes Act II. Rhadames has come back a conqueror from the war against the Ethiopians, dragging his captives along in chains, and he is greeted by a thrilling Chorus of Victory. For this paean of triumph, Verdi wrote parts for first and second sopranos, three different groups of tenors, and three different groups of basses. As if this were not enough, he subdivided his groups so that at one point thirteen different melodic lines are being sung simultaneously. The effect is electric, but the voltage would drop sharply if the members of the chorus came in at the wrong time, sang even slightly out of tune, or lost the rhythm. This scene requires considerable work, and the listener who feels his scalp tingle with excitement rarely realizes how much rehearsal by chorus and chorus master was needed to create his emotional response.

There are other opportunities for the chorus to make itself felt: in the first scene of the opera, for example, where the men appear as priests and ministers of Pharaoh, and in the second scene, in the temple, when the women sing offstage. These relatively simple scenes must be brought up to the same standard of perfection as the others, and some of them will be run through every day as long as *Aïda* is being rehearsed. At the same time,

Artists rehearse wherever a stage is available. To prepare Girl of the Golden West *for the San Francisco Opera season, the singers use the stage of Piper's Opera House, an old theatre in Virginia City.*

the chorus is also mastering scenes from the other operas that are being prepared.

Meanwhile, the choreographer has made himself completely familiar with the score, has finished his studies of ancient Egyptian painting and sculpture, and knows what the projected sets of the opera will be. But he cannot plan dances without taking into consideration the layout of the stage, even though the first few rehearsals will take place in the ballet studio.

He may arrange the dances of the priestesses in the temple scene first. These dances, like the choral music in this scene, are part of the religious ceremonies, and the choreography must communicate a religious quality. The corps de ballet, wearing leotards and ballet slippers, joins the choreographer, a pianist, and the ballet mistress. From time to time a conductor will appear to make sure that the dances are staged in the right tempo. There are several dances in *Aïda* in addition to those in the temple scene, among the more important being the slaves' dance in the chambers of Pharaoh's daughter, and the victory procession. The ballet faces the same problem as the chorus and orchestra—a limited number of rehearsals for any one opera. There are other operas with ballets to be rehearsed.

After all the dances have been learned, the corps and the ballet soloists rehearse on stage with piano accompaniment, again with a conductor on hand. Then they join the rest of the company in a run-through of the entire opera before dress rehearsal.

In the meantime, the leading singers and their alternates have been meeting with conductor and director for musical and staging rehearsals of the different scenes in which they appear. For example, in the final scene of Act III, Aïda and her father, Amonasro, the defeated Ethiopian king, sing a stirring duet in which he demands that Aïda obtain the Egyptian military plans from Rhadames. Rhadames appears for a tryst with Aïda, decides to flee with her, and unwittingly betrays the Egyptian strategy to Amonasro, who had hidden at Rhadames' approach. Amneris overhears, from the temple where she is awaiting Rhadames. She and Ramphis, the High Priest, have Rhadames seized by the guards as a traitor, while Aïda and her father escape. All this musical plotting and counterplotting require careful timing by soloists and orchestra.

The soloists' rehearsal periods are just as carefully scheduled as all others. Each artist is asked to appear at a specific time, so that he will not have to sit around while other artists are working. Aïda and Amonasro, for example, will rehearse in a small

An artists' studio rehearsal of Don Giovanni *by Mozart, at the San Francisco Opera.* Standing from left to right: *Lorenzo Alvary, Kurt Herbert Adler, Sena Jurinac, Richard Lewis, Leontyne Price, Mino Yahia.* Seated: *Conductor Leopold Ludwig* (with raised arm); at his left, *Assistant Conductor Marcel Frank;* behind them, *Joan Marie Moynagh.*

studio at 10:00 A.M., to be joined at 11:00 by Rhadames and, forty-five minutes later, by Amneris and her father. At these scenes, the director will sketch the stage action and tell them how he expects them to move, while the conductor who is to lead the performances will work on the musical interpretation he wants. After a time the rehearsal will move to the stage, where the various scenes and movements will be blocked in more completely.

Until the entire company is familiar with the action, only a few props are placed on the stage. Rehearsals with full sets, in costume, and with the orchestra come later. Such rehearsals can be very expensive, as the number of rehearsal hours that singers, musicians, dancers, and stage crews may work is arranged with various unions. They are therefore kept to a minimum, and their timing is carefully planned. To avoid the payment of overtime, all stage rehearsals start and stop close to the minute of their scheduled hours.

The lighting director has discussed the question of lights with the director and designers, and by the time of the first stage rehearsal knows approximately what he will do. He sits in the auditorium and, by means of an intercommunication system hooked up to the various electrical posts, keeps up a running commentary on the lights that are to be used at each stage of the action. All these cues are carefully noted on the lighting plot, which will be used for all performances of the opera.

The director has been busy all along with rehearsals of the soloists and chorus. Now, at the final rehearsals on stage with the entire company, he coordinates all the movements, changes those which for one reason or another do not please him or the conductor, and stands in different places throughout the theatre the better to judge how the performers look from different angles, now that they are in costume and the sets are in place.

The conductor makes his final adjustments in interpretation, tempo, and the volume of sound he wants from the singers on the stage and the orchestra in the pit. The assistant conductor in the prompter's box notes these changes in his copy of the score.

The stage and costume designers attend to such last-minute details as the shortening of a train on a costume that otherwise might get caught in some part of the set, or the rearrangement of furnishings on the stage to give a more striking appearance, or merely to be less in the way of the soloists. The choreographer runs through his dances on stage. His dancers may find that with a full cast and sets crowding them, the stage is not as roomy as they had thought. Also, they have the additional problem of adjusting to performance with the orchestra. They have to respond to cues from string and wind instruments instead of from the piano which has until then accompanied their rehearsals.

As a result of all the activities going on, the opportunity for conflicts and clashes of opinion is unlimited. Mistakes are made by singers and eagerly pointed out by conductors, or vice versa. If not made, they are often imagined. Much rehearsal time is devoted to the airing of differences of opinion and, to those who do not take part in them, the arguments seem a silly waste of time.

Silly or not, they must be settled. The decision made after an argument may not be the best one, but at least it should be definite, and should leave no one in doubt as to what to do. Unfortunately, each argument may touch off a series of other arguments. If the conductor loses to a star soloist, he may seek to salve his pride with victory over a less important singer, who looks in his turn for a victim of still lower rank.

The final dress rehearsal is supposed to be conducted as if it were an actual performance, complete in every detail, including a small audience composed of members of the company who are not in *Aïda*. This is scheduled several days before the opera is presented to the public. Ideally, a dress rehearsal should be run through without interruptions and without repeats, in order to maintain the illusion of a performance. In practice, because there are seldom enough previous rehearsals, both repeats and interruptions occur.

If something goes wrong, if, for instance, a section of the chorus, that is unaccustomed to the new scenery, marches in through the wrong gate, the mistake must be corrected at once. The soloists may be in the wrong places on the stage, the conductor may object to the way they or the chorus sound, the lighting may be unsatisfactory, bathing the soloists in colored lights that make their costumes turn gray. Someone may object to the decrepit spears the soldiers carry. Why weren't new spears made to replace the old ones, or at least why weren't the old ones painted over? In the temple scene at the end of the first act, where prayers for victory are ascending to the gods and incense is being burnt, there may be either too much or too little smoke.

The entire opera house is alive with stage hands, experts of various kinds, and representatives of the management, all trying to make up their minds how the opera will look and sound at the opening, and all searching for flaws. Their movements may distract the performers, but this, too, is part of rehearsal, for professionals must become accustomed to distractions. The less the experts like what has been done the more they will interfere, and the less chance there is that the dress rehearsal will look and sound like a real performance.

By all the demands of common sense, therefore, there should be at least two full dress rehearsals, or else more preliminary rehearsals. But need for economy conflicts with common sense, except in a few relatively wealthy opera houses abroad, where costs of production are much less, and a new production may be rehearsed until the conductor and management are satisfied that it is ready for performance. In this country, the actual dress rehearsal usually represents at best a half-finished performance.

There have been a few striking exceptions. When the first performance of Alban Berg's modern opera, *Wozzek,* was being prepared, it was obvious that the usual pattern of rehearsals would not suffice. The opera took only one and a half hours to perform, but the music was so complicated and unfamiliar that at first neither the orchestra nor the soloists could make head or tail of it. Two casts of principal singers began work on *Wozzek* a year before the opening. At least thirty rehearsals were required before they reached the point where they could sing the parts, and twenty more to attain the desired dramatic effects. The orchestra required twelve orchestral readings alone, and eight stage readings. This number of rehearsals was unprecedented at the Metropolitan.

All sorts of difficulties cropped up. There were many notes or passages in *falsetto,* a high-pitched unnatural type of singing which is difficult to control. There were passages in *sprechstimme* (speech melody), a method of intonation intermediate between speech and singing. In general the singers had to learn their parts note by note instead of melody by melody. Often, the singers had no support from the orchestra, so that they lacked simple cues as to when to come in. The presence of two stage bands did not make rehearsals simpler. One band was used backstage, the other onstage during a café scene. At one point the orchestra in the pit had to play in 5/4 time, a rather difficult rhythm, against the stage band playing in 3/4 time, the latter accompanied into the bargain by an out-of-tune piano.

The orchestra might have been forgiven for being bewildered. But it should be noted that the composer knew exactly the effect he wanted, and that the final production was highly effective.

In the past, dress rehearsals have been distinguished by the presence of critics. As this is written, this is no longer true, but the situation may change again. Most performers have no great prejudice against critics, but they have objected strongly to one unfortunate aspect of their attendance at dress rehearsals. As the opera usually ends at too late an hour of the opening night for the critic to write a review that will make the next morning's edition, it has been customary to base the review on the dress rehearsal instead of on the performance that the audience actually sees, and merely to note, if changes should occur, alterations in the cast, replacement of one conductor by another, and so on. This procedure has sometimes led to unfavorable notices which, to an audience that has enjoyed a first-rate opening performance, have been mystifying and incomprehensible. By barring critics from dress rehearsals, the management hopes to ensure reviews based on the actual performance.

Even the best dress rehearsals, without an interruption or repeat, is not like the performance itself. Because singers and dancers realize that mistakes cannot be avoided completely, because they know that these are to some extent expected, and because the audience is so limited, some of the performances are not up to the highest standards. A soprano, for instance, will very sensibly not strain her voice at rehearsal. It requires the inspiration of an actual audience to raise performances to their highest level, and to extract from those on stage the best they are capable of. It is all very well to have other singers and management out front, and even the critics, but it is usually only for a genuine audience that professionals give their best.

opera abroad 13

FROM ITS BIRTHPLACE in Italy, opera spread all over the world, so that we can now hear *Die Meistersinger* sung by a Japanese cast and accompanied by a Japanese orchestra in Tokyo, or *Madama Butterfly* with an international cast and an Argentine orchestra in Buenos Aires. Nevertheless, opera in Asia and South America, as well as in our own continent, has not yet become an art for a large part of the people, as it has long been in Europe.

In Italy, France, Germany, Switzerland, Austria, Czechoslavakia, Yugoslavia, Sweden, England, the Soviet Union, and other European countries, opera is a form of entertainment that can be enjoyed not only in the largest cities, but in relatively small ones as well. In these countries there are several hundred professional groups, some with their own theatres, others with theatres which they share with spoken drama or ballet. These groups are partially or wholly subsidized by the national or local governments. The subsidies may be as much as a million dollars a year, as for an opera house in Vienna, or only a few thousand, for a small city opera house. For an entire country like Germany they may amount to twenty million dollars a year—not a large sum compared to the money spent for trivial or harmful purposes. But such subsidies assure opera's survival.

The health of opera in Europe, however, is not due only to these subsidies. People attend performances for many reasons, first of all because they enjoy a drama told in music. In European opera the story has always been an important part of the production, as we can see from the general insistence that the libretto be translated into the language of the country in which the opera is performed. Germans want to hear *The Marriage of Figaro* in German, despite the fact that Mozart composed it originally for a libretto in Italian, and that the music so carefully reflects the spirit of the Italian words. In the same way, Italians will grant that a translation of *Boris Godunov* into their own language must to some extent destroy the harmony between the music and the Russian words. But the ability to understand what is going on upon the stage appears to them a gain worth the sacrifice.

Opera-goers of all nations enjoy the same things in opera, but not to the same degree. The emphasis on one factor or another is part of a national tradition which changes only slowly. The French, as we have seen, have stressed the need for ballet, and have never permitted the singers completely to distort an opera, as the Italians have done. The Germans have insisted on the importance of the staging as a whole in bringing out dramatic values, especially since Wagner set the example at Bayreuth. The Italians also emphasized dramatic values, but in the past were usually satisfied to achieve them almost entirely by musical means. Ever since Toscanini, however, there has been greater unity in Italian opera. The Czechs, the Belgians, the Dutch, and the Swiss all have emphasized different aspects of operatic production at different times. The present trend everywhere appears to be toward integration of all elements into a unified production.

In addition to the other factors leading to the popularity of

The interior of the Festspielhaus in Bayreuth, built as a showcase for Wagnerian music dramas.

opera abroad, we must not forget the importance of local tradition, and the association of great names with individual cities and theatres. If New Yorkers and Pennsylvanians point with pride to the numerous houses where George Washington slept, then the Czechs point with even more pride to the theatre in Prague where Mozart staged the first performance of his *Don Giovanni,* and Parisians boast that Bizet's *Carmen* was first produced in their own Opéra Comique. The countries of Europe are rich in traditions of this kind, and these traditions do help to bring people to the opera houses.

If we can learn any lesson from the history of art in general and of opera in particular, it is that no new art form becomes genuinely popular until it adapts itself to the customs of a country. Opera did not take root in France until it had incorporated the French ballet and the French style of recitative, or in Germany until it had stimulated German composers to compose operas in German. In England, as we have seen, *The Beggar's Opera,* based on native songs and a native theme, almost drove Italian opera out altogether. Handel wrote better music than can be found in *The Beggar's Opera,* but his operas were financial failures by comparison.

In recent years it has become customary to maintain national and local traditions by annual summer festivals. Many of these festivals are frankly aimed at attracting tourists, and their number has increased to such an extent that they have begun to compete with each other. The Wagner festival at Bayreuth remains outstanding, as does the Glyndebourne Opera Festival in Great Britain (performances have been given in different cities), the Edinburgh Festival, and the Salzburg Festival in Austria. Of somewhat lesser importance are the Munich Festival, the Vienna Festival, the Holland Festival, and the Maggio Musicale in Florence. Some of these, and other festivals, give purely musical or dramatic works as well as opera. An opera-lover who does not mind travelling can now see and hear opera throughout the year.

The quality of what he sees and hears will vary tremendously. To some extent this is due to the difference between a country that maintains one or two professional opera companies, such as Holland or Argentina, and one that maintains a large number, such as Italy or Germany. In Holland, for example, even a large company operates almost in isolation. It has no suitable training ground for singers, stage directors, or conductors, and it is often forced to import its artists from abroad. Where there is a network of opera companies, small and large, the small companies can afford to experiment with people who have ability but have not yet acquired experience. By giving them reasonable security, and by testing them in one production after another, it can help develop their talents.

The large companies, on the other hand, can depend on the small ones as a training ground. This need not be at the latter's expense, for along with a network of opera houses goes a network of music schools and conservatories, where conductors and directors teach and in turn learn what is going on in the younger musical generation. The large companies may be able to recommend to the small ones singers and conductors who have great potential and need only a few years of experience. The small companies thus benefit from the talents of capable people they might overlook, the schools and conservatories benefit from the presence of a professional faculty and from the possibilities these open to their students, and the students benefit most of all from the opportunity to acquire training and to go on to better positions.

It should be noted that government support of opera in Europe has never depended greatly on the nature of the government. In a number of European capitals before World War I, Imperial or Royal Theatres and Operas were supported by kings and emperors. After the war, when a number of republics replaced the empires, support was continued, although the name of the theatre was usually changed. There was often a change of emphasis in the nature of the play or opera produced, so that opera houses formerly run for the benefit of the nobility, with commoners relegated to the worst seats, were transformed into popular institutions.

There have been other factors in the popularity of European opera, not least among them the generally low admission prices to the smaller theatres. In the past, European wages and salaries in almost every trade and profession have generally been far below those in America, and although the gap has been partly

The arena at Verona, Italy, where thousands can attend opera performances at modest prices.

closed, it is still less expensive to produce opera, or any other form of theatre, for that matter, in Europe than in the United States. This has not prevented opera companies from losing money, but it has permitted them to stage many more rehearsals than is customary in the United States, so that the deficit at the end of a season is modest, and easily made up by government subsidy.

To the young artist, all this has meant wider opportunities, for the greater the number of rehearsals the less important it is to learn everything rapidly and superficially, and the smaller the advantage of a perhaps fading but experienced talent over a young and untried one. The fact that salaries for inexperienced artists are low also helps ensure that the newcomer will be given a chance. And as the audience itself is accustomed to receive low salaries and pay low prices, tickets for first-class performances usually run about a third to a half the prices of corresponding American tickets. There are, however, a few exceptions, such as La Scala in Milan, and some of the festivals, where tickets are expensive.

Because he ordinarily pays less for a ticket, the European opera-goer is willing to attend more frequently without the lure of a new star. Having been admitted for fifty cents or a dollar, he does not share the attitude of the resentful patron in this country, who often thinks: "I've paid twenty dollars for this pair of tickets. This show isn't worth all that money!" Where tickets are reasonable in price, the patron stops thinking of a performance in terms of money value. Moreover, he can be more relaxed in his attitude, for he usually does not have to make season reservations, as he does for the Metropolitan Opera in New York, and for many community operas in the United States. Attending opera can be a much more casual affair in Europe than in the United States, and this helps it to remain entertainment.

The fact that European opera houses are built according to a different pattern also adds to the enjoyment of European patrons. In important theatres there is more stage space, which contributes to the efficiency of production by allowing room for the use of revolving stages, storage of sets, and so on. At the same time, with a few exceptions, which include a number of amphitheatres, there is a smaller auditorium, so that a patron can see well from almost every seat. We must marvel at the patience of some of the patrons of our own Metropolitan Opera, who for years have paid their money for seats from which the singers have looked like puppets on a stage, distorted because of the sharpness of the angle of vision, and sometimes hidden by pillars into the bargain. It is to be hoped that the move to Lincoln Center will change this. There are bad seats in European theatres, of course, but not so many of them, especially in the small houses. They were plentiful, though, in the days of court theatres, when everything was arranged for the benefit of the royal patron and the common people were pleased to be permitted inside at all, without being so unreasonable as to demand a view of the stage. But when the people traded in their governments for new models, they remodeled their theatres as well.

The chief objection to a small theatre is a simple one: by decreasing the number of paying patrons it decreases the income from an opera company and makes it all the more difficult to make ends meet. This is a less serious objection in Europe, especially as far as the numerous local opera companies are concerned, not only because of the generally low salaries for every one from orchestral musician to carpenter or electrician, but because the star system is either non-existent or less well developed. Two stars, each with a salary of a thousand dollars a performance, would create a serious deficit for a small European opera company.

Stars do appear, of course, in the important opera houses and festivals, and their salaries have gone up because of the competition with American opera, but in general they still receive less for European than for American performances.

For all these reasons—the native tradition of great composers, great operas, and great theatres, the insistence on opera as a drama which can be understood, the emphasis on integration of the arts, the extensive network of theatres and schools, the low cost of opera, the help by government subsidy, and the consideration for the comfort and convenience of the audience—European opera is in a relatively flourishing state. It has its problems, but they are not often matters of life and death, as they so frequently are for American opera.

american opera 14

In some ways, American opera is far ahead of where it was forty or fifty years ago, in the period to which people with long but limited memories look back so fondly. Audiences have changed for the better. Only on the first night of a new season, or during the first appearance of a highly publicized star does a large part of the audience come to see or let itself be seen. The singers now know far more about music and acting than the sopranos and tenors of two generations ago. More emphasis has been placed on dramatic values, and a greater effort has been made to integrate music, story, scenery, and physical action.

There is more opera to be seen and heard. New York City now has two professional companies instead of one, and so has San Francisco. Many members of the new audience, attracted by radio and TV broadcasts, and by recordings, have begun to organize and support local opera companies, both professional and amateur. The growth of amateur companies, in music schools, colleges, and communities, has been remarkable.

That is the bright side of the picture. The other side becomes clearer when we contrast the condition of opera in this country with that of Europe. Where more than a hundred companies in Europe have full seasons of opera for up to ten months a year, only one opera house in the United States, the Metropolitan, has what may be called a full season, and that is for about six months. The New York City Opera, on the other hand, gives only a month of performances in the fall and another in the spring, scheduling its productions so as to overlap the Metropolitan schedule as little as possible.

Outside of New York, professional performances are even more infrequent, except for Chicago, where the Lyric Opera has a season of seven weeks or more. The San Francisco Opera Company schedules about a month of performances in the fall, and the other San Francisco company, the Cosmopolitan Opera, schedules only about a week of opera, the exact number of performances depending on the state of the budget, the availability of stars and conductors, and other factors. The Pittsburgh Opera gives perhaps ten performances, the Philadelphia Grand Opera Company a small number also, despite some financial support from the city of Philadelphia. The St. Louis Municipal Opera gives three months of performances outdoors each summer, but these are of musical comedy and operetta, not of grand opera, while the St. Paul Civic Opera Association schedules a few serious operas and some musicals. Cincinnati has been fighting valiantly, and so far successfully, to continue its summer season in the zoo, but the total number of performances given is from twenty-five to thirty.

This almost exhausts the list of professional opera performances in the United States. We might perhaps add several so-called operatic companies that produce chiefly musical comedies, and a few privately owned companies that give occasional performances in New York City or on the road. In addition, both the Metropolitan and the New York City Opera go on tour, although it must be admitted that the performances they give on the road do not always represent opera at its best. For one thing, the unsuitability of the theatres—especially the lack of stage space—makes it necessary to skimp on ballet and crowd scenes, creates difficulties in lighting, and leads to generally inferior productions. Because of the tremendous cost of moving an opera company, both the Metropolitan and the New York City Opera lose money on tour.

As all professional opera companies face the same problems to somewhat different degrees, there is little opportunity for the young artist. The season is short, rehearsal time is limited because of financial considerations, money is difficult to raise, and audiences do not acquire the habit of attendance. Hence experienced singers and conductors are needed to ensure a reasonably smooth production, and to attract the audience.

The uncertainty of existence of the company from year to year prevents the formation of strong ties with schools and conservatories. The Metropolitan Opera has friendly relations with the Juilliard School of Music in New York City, and other music schools in the country, but even these are not close enough to permit newcomers to secure professional experience. The result is that many singers, directors, and conductors must be imported from Europe, and even American singers, chosen for the Metropolitan, often gain their experience in Europe.

The financial problems involved in producing professional opera are so formidable that every group must have its sponsors who contribute from their own pockets and also spend considerable time in fund-raising. At one time the Metropolitan Opera operated at a profit. The surplus built up during the early years of the century vanished during the 1930s, however, and since then the company, like all other professional opera companies in the United States, has made a habit of losing money.

The condition of amateur opera is on the whole a much healthier one. Throughout the country, in workshops, music schools, churches, colleges, high schools, and even in the United States Army, there are some eight hundred opera-producing groups. They are found in Hawaii and Alaska, in Texas and Utah, on the East Coast from Maine to Florida and on the

West Coast in Washington, Oregon, and California. Some put on a single opera and then expire; others produce a number of operas each year. Productions range from miserable to excellent, although at their best they are weak in great voices, and cannot compete with a good professional production.

Amateur performances have been condemned by some professionals because of their inevitable limitations, and there has been some question as to whether they are beneficial at all. Their orchestras are skimpy, or sometimes are replaced altogether by one or two pianos; scenery is generally limited; and the ballet and chorus, not to speak of the principal singers, are very likely to commit blunders.

Amateurs may retort that professionals are in no position to throw stones. If Mozart did not write *The Marriage of Figaro* to be performed by singers to the accompaniment of two pianos, neither did he write it for a hundred-piece orchestra. Where amateurs cannot help skimping, professionals who should know better become over-elaborate. The scenery has rarely been one of the glories of the Metropolitan, nor are examples of confusion and bewilderment on its stage unknown, despite the presence of a prompter and a multitude of assistants.

Mistakes and failures are certainly more forgivable in amateur opera, especially as it is not intended to compete with the professional brand. It is meant to train performers and production staff, to encourage new composers and give them a proving ground, and to attract new audiences that have never before had a chance to become interested in opera. Whatever its weaknesses, it represents an active instead of passive approach, from which opera can only benefit. And sometimes the amateur's very inexperience stands him in good stead. The professional knows so well what will work that he limits his point of view. The amateur, in his ignorance, does things that shouldn't work—and sometimes brings them off successfully.

It is well to remember that since the days when opera itself began as an amateur invention, people who have had difficulty getting into the professional theatre have made important contributions to it. Serious American drama dates from the production of O'Neill's early plays by the Provincetown Playhouse, an off-Broadway group. And as the professional theatre on Broadway continues to decline year after year, amateur groups across the country flourish as never before. Some twenty-five hundred colleges and universities and twenty thousand high schools produce plays, and there are from five to ten thousand community theatres of all kinds. Together they put on possibly thirty-five thousand productions a year, and play to an audience of fifty million. This is far beyond anything Broadway or off-Broadway now does.

Opera is more difficult to produce than spoken drama, and amateur producing groups are fewer in number. Whatever the faults, the chief weakness of amateur groups lies not within themselves but in the professional companies outside them. Amateur opera, in particular, would be more vigorous if professional opera in this country were in reasonably good health. In Europe the music school and conservatory productions of opera benefit from the help of large numbers of professionals. In this country, professional opera is itself looking for help.

One of the important differences between amateur and professional opera is that the former can be understood by its audiences. During the 1960-61 season, for instance, the Metropolitan Opera gave twenty-four operas, of which fourteen were in Italian, four German, one French, and only five in English. Even if amateur groups were capable of performing in Italian or German, their audiences would not be interested. Of necessity, they sing in English, and it is possible that professional companies would benefit from doing the same thing. Among the

Met's audiences, and for that matter among its non-Italian singers, few understand the shades of meaning of an Italian libretto as well as an Italian peasant does. Most do not understand Italian at all. They follow the action with the help of a synopsis or translation which they have studied beforehand, and the singers might just as well be singing nonsense syllables.

To many people, translation of an opera into English means a loss of magic. That it also means a gain in understanding, in interest, and in dramatic power, is immaterial to them, for they do not think of an opera as drama. Only when opera is sung in a language that can be understood, English for Americans, or Italian for Italians, must it be thought of in this way. It becomes clearer than ever then that some librettos are old-fashioned and depend on dramatic clichés that have lost their effectiveness. If anything is to contribute to the growth of a healthy operatic art, it must be dissatisfaction with what was done in the past or with what is customary in Italy or Germany, but is quite unsuitable here. Such dissatisfaction opens the way for the composition of new American operas.

In fact, a number of such new operas have been written, many of them aimed at first performance by amateur groups, especially in schools. Kurt Weill's *Down in the Valley,* a short one-act opera with libretto by Arnold Sundgaard, was first performed in 1948 by students at Indiana University (with a professional conductor and stage director, however) and has been popular with amateur groups ever since. Also popular have been such operas by Douglas Moore as *The Devil and Daniel Webster, Giants in the Earth,* and *The Ballad of Baby Doe.* Other composers who have already attained recognition, like Gian-Carlo Menotti and English composer Benjamin Britten, and a number of young composers previously unknown, have also found an opportunity in amateur opera.

Not all the new operas have first been performed by amateur groups. The New York City Opera, in 1961 alone, gave first performances of Douglas Moore's *The Wings of the Dove,* based on the novel by Henry James, and of Robert Ward's *The Crucible,* based on the play by Arthur Miller. In addition, the New York City Opera has given first New York City performances of operas first presented elsewhere.

We have seen how near to impossible it is for a young composer to write for the large and famous opera companies. The difficulties do not vanish, but they shrink to less monstrous proportions when a composer writes for amateur companies, or for the less exalted professional organizations. Many of these groups welcome short operas, they want relatively simple arias that

The Ballad of Baby Doe, *an American opera by Douglas Moore, as performed by the New York City Opera.*

can be sung well by inexperienced performers, they minimize the problem of finding good instrumentalists by having small orchestras, and they insist on dramatic stories told in a language with which the composer himself is familiar. Both the physical labor and the exhaustive creative demands involved in writing an opera are reduced, as is the expense of copying parts.

Composers who would have been foolish to devote two years of their lives to writing an opera for which there was no chance of production are eager to write works for which an audience is waiting. The amateur companies pay only trifling royalties, but performances are repeated often by many groups, and the reputation gained from the composition of a popular opera opens doors on which the composer might otherwise knock in vain.

May we again recall that this is a return to the first days of opera, when the play was the thing, the music was simple and singable, the orchestra small, and the scenery limited? Composers and audiences alike have learned much since then, and they realize that there are many legitimate forms of opera and many different ways of writing them. The best way is the one most suited to the resources on which the composer can count and the audience for which he writes.

It is very likely that the aristocratic Florentine audiences for which the first operatic composers wrote would have been highly impressed by such works as *Down in the Valley.* The simple story would have moved them, the strange melodies and harmonies would have pleased, and the use of English, which they didn't understand, might have lent that touch of glamour which so many audiences have enjoyed in Italian opera. Our own student groups, by the way, are fond of producing a number of simple operas from somewhat later periods, such as *The Beggar's Opera,* and Pergolesi's *La Serva Padrona,* the latter in

English translation, of course. They have good reason for feeling close to these particular operatic ancestors.

We have so far said nothing in the present chapter about the American musical comedies or operettas which have on occasion been called folk operas. Although they are a form of opera, their problems are different from those of either grand opera or *opéra comique*. Produced for profit and sold as high-priced entertainment, they are revised during the tryout period with producer, director, and others having more to say than the composer. They therefore tend to be highly polished and, if successful, highly entertaining, but the music plays only an auxiliary role. Comedy, sensational dancing, and "production numbers" are more important. If a few musical comedies and operettas have become part of our art and culture, they have done so despite the manner in which they have been produced, and largely because of a talented author and composer working under difficult conditions.

The musical comedies worth remembering as highly skilled art include *Oklahoma!*, *Finian's Rainbow*, *West Side Story*, *My Fair Lady*, *South Pacific*, and a small number of others. *Porgy and Bess* remains a fascinating folk opera. Such works are too elaborate for production by a small amateur group, though some have been given in high schools. But the influence they have exerted, and continue to exert, is felt in the music now being written by American composers.

For a time it was hoped that television and the movies would add a great deal to the growth of opera in this country. But television productions are so expensive that only a few performances have been given in any season, while equally few film versions have been made of famous operas. The television networks have commissioned a small number of original operas, but have found the prospect too unrewarding financially. So far as we are aware, no companies either here or abroad have commissioned original operas for filming.

The chief hope of opera in the United States, therefore, remains the increasing number of school and community opera workshops. Large organizations such as the Ford Foundation have begun to help, and the Central Opera Service sponsored by the National Council of the Metropolitan Opera Association acts to inform and help the various small companies.

The people connected with these companies are well aware of the problems they face. They themselves have such small budgets that their financial needs may be easy to meet, but they know that the weaknesses of professional opera in the United States sooner or later are reflected in them, and it is the professional companies that need assurance of financial support. Lack of money is the root of most of the evil in opera.

What can be done about it? Professional opera is so expensive to produce that admission fees cannot possibly pay the costs. Throughout its life, the Metropolitan Opera has had to rely on a small number of private sponsors, and in the past thirty years or so has asked for support from its radio and television audiences as well. If contributions from all over the United States can barely keep the Met alive, there is little hope that they will maintain professional companies in other cities as well. It has been suggested that large corporations might take over the burden, and in fact commercial sponsors have helped to defray the costs of broadcasts. But there is always the question whether the sponsor will continue to pay from year to year. So far, few large companies have indicated an abiding interest in opera.

The only alternative appears to be subsidy at either the city, state, or federal level. A number of cities in the United States grant tax exemptions, and New York City permits the New York City Opera to use a theatre rent-free. But such minor aid is not enough to permit full-scale operation of a thoroughly professional group. Much more is needed to support opera throughout the United States.

Many people in the theatre and opera have concluded that government subsidies at the local or federal level are the only solution. European experience with government support of the arts indicates that the expected difficulties, such as government interference, often do not materialize. When they do, there is trouble—but no more than can be expected when a board of trustees interferes in the management of an opera, or when management interferes with the conductor.

Government interference need not be harmful. It was government interference that saved the Metropolitan's 1961-1962 season when the management had already announced cancellation because of a dispute with the Musician's Union. The chief difficulty that opera has faced so far is, in fact, the reluctance of the government to interfere in its financial affairs.

Before government support can be obtained, opera companies must reconsider their responsibilities. If they expect public money, they must serve the public. This means greater emphasis on productions a new opera-going public can be expected to understand and feel close to. It means lower ticket prices. For those who fear that it also means a lowering of standards, we can again refer to the experience of European opera houses, whose standards, by and large, are at least equal to those of American companies.

What operas can American opera-goers be expected to feel close to? Certainly the great works of the past, from Rossini's *Barber of Seville* and Mozart's *Don Giovanni* to Puccini's *Madama Butterfly* and Moussorgsky's *Boris Godunov*. When professional opera is no longer the monopoly of one company, many of these operas can be given in their original language as well as English, so that the public may have its chance to decide which version it prefers.

There is no such thing as healthy opera, however, without the encouragement of new composers. The national and patriotic themes of the past can still serve them as inspiration. When we realize that a Polish opera like Moniuzko's *Halka,* and a Hungarian work like Ferenc Erkel's *Bánk-Bán,* are still alive in Poland and Hungary after more than a century, even though little known elsewhere, it should be clear that an American opera about Lincoln or Washington or Daniel Boone might also succeed, provided it were based on a dramatic libretto and had first-rate music. But the modern composer has his choice of new themes as well, such as the old composers never imagined. No longer interested in the sorrows of mythical kings and queens, he may write a "space opera," as the Swedish composer Karl-Birger Blomdahl did in his *Aniara*—the story of people in a space ship fleeing from the earth. Produced in Stockholm and Edinburgh, and then recorded, it suggests some of the themes of a future in which life has caught up with fantasy.

Only a few operas by American composers have been produced at the Metropolitan, and these have not been very successful. If there were as many as a dozen American opera companies with full seasons, the situation would change. It would be possible to produce many more operas, and the chance of producing good ones would increase. Recall the thousands of forgotten operas that were produced all over Italy, Germany, and France in the seventeenth and eighteenth centuries and are not worth reviving—and then recall that these thousands led to the writing of operas that are still alive. Hundreds of composers wrote pot-boilers about Orpheus, that two great works might survive. If in twenty years, government subsidy of opera leads not only to popular enjoyment of the classics but to the production of one great work, as well as a dozen operas worth performing, now and then, the people would have a right to feel that they had received their money's worth.

If professional opera could be produced in many cities for a full season, if the theatres in which they were given could be utilized for the best musical comedies, operettas, and for spoken plays as well, many financial problems would be eased. Musicians who could count on a full season of work, and even more important, on working year after year, without the constant fear of having their jobs disappear, might conceivably be less insistent on a higher weekly salary. A good part of the difficulty between management and musicians, actors, singers, stagehands, and other people connected with the theatre comes from the continual shrinkage in the number of jobs.

Do people really want opera enough for the government to support it to the extent of millions of dollars a year? People *have* been supporting opera, sending in hundreds of thousands of dollars yearly to the Metropolitan Opera alone. But most of the contributors have little chance to see opera at the Met. Certainly their support would be greater for an opera company they felt was their own. When the Metropolitan threatened to close down in the fall of 1961, critics and audiences hailed the alertness of a television station that scheduled the showing of a dozen movies of famous operas. This would indicate that there is a genuine demand for opera.

The feeling that government subsidy is needed has been slowly growing over the years. If support does not come, fairly soon professional opera in this country will face even more difficult times than in the past, and so will amateur opera.

Meanwhile, many of the operas that are still being produced are things of beauty, well worth seeing and hearing. Our national life would be poorer without them.

Glossary of Operatic Terms

ARIA *(Italian)*—a solo vocal piece within the opera, usually a show piece for the singer.

BEL CANTO *(Italian)*—an Italian style of singing, emphasizing beautiful tone and vocal agility. Used to denote a method of singing.

BRINDISI *(Italian)*—a drinking song common in many Italian operas.

CABALETTA *(Italian)*—a short aria with repetitions and variations. In Verdi's operas, the *cabaletta* is the final rapid section of a long and elaborate aria or duet.

CANZONETTA *(Italian)*—a short solo song, less elaborate and less dramatic than the aria.

CAVATINA *(Italian)*—a very simple and melodic song without the vocal embellishments of the aria.

COLORATURA—not an Italian word, but derived from the German word *koloratur.* The Italian name is *fioritura,* flowery style. It denotes florid ornamentation in vocal music.

COMIC OPERA—see OPERA BUFFA.

DUETTO *(Italian)*—A vocal piece for two singers.

GRAND OPERA—originally a French term which properly means opera of which the libretto is entirely set to music. While this is still generally true of Italian opera, the term has come to mean many different things so that, according to today's practice, it is really not definable.

LEITMOTIV (*German*)—a musical theme used throughout an opera to identify a character or plot situation. Although *leitmotivs* were used by composers before Wagner, his extensive use of the device has identified the term with Wagnerian music drama.

MESSA DI VOCE (*Italian*)—the gradual swelling and diminution of a long-held single vocal note.

MEZZA VOCE *(Italian)*—singing with half the usual power of the voice.

OPERA BUFFA *(Italian)* or OPERA BOUFFE *(French)*—comic opera, not necessarily farce, in which spoken dialogue is introduced. The Gilbert and Sullivan operas are examples. However, it may also be opera entirely set to music, like Verdi's *Falstaff*. The term is Italian in origin, French by adoption, but is not used consistently. Italian *opera buffa* usually uses *recitativo secco* rather than spoken dialogue.

OPÉRA COMIQUE—Does not mean comic opera. The subject may be tragic as in *Carmen*. Originally meant opera in which spoken dialogue is used so is similar to comic opera in that way, but now some operas without spoken dialogue are included, so, like grand opera, it is no longer really definable.

OPERA SERIA *(Italian)*—"serious" as distinguished from "comic" opera, devoted to dramatic or tragic themes.

OPERETTA—light opera, containing spoken dialogue and set musical numbers such as arias, comedy songs, and duets.

OVERTURE—a piece of orchestral music that introduces the opera.

PRELUDE or VORSPIEL *(German)*—orchestral music that introduces the opera, but is shorter and less formal in structure than the overture. The term is often used synonymously for overture in opera.

QUARTETTO *(Italian)*—a musical number for four voices.

RECITATIVO *(Italian)*—a form of vocal composition that resembles declamatory speech, and permits greater rhythmic latitude to the singer. Often precedes a formal aria. *Recitativo secco* (dry recitative) utilizes a very simple accompaniment of chords, played by either the piano or harpsichord. *Recitativo accompagnato* employs the orchestra for its accompaniment, which is fuller in sound than the *secco*.

ROMANZA *(Italian)* or ROMANCE—a solo song, so named at the discretion of the composer because of the nature of the lyrics. It is shorter, more romantic, and less dramatic than the aria.

SCENA *(Italian)*—in opera, a long vocal solo in several movements, containing recitative and arias.

SERIOUS OPERA—see OPERA SERIA.

SESTETTO *(Italian)*—a piece for six singers. The sextet from *Lucia di Lammermoor* is a famous example.

SINGSPIEL *(German)*—a dramatic musical work containing fairly equal portions of spoken text and singing. In many ways, the equivalent of comic opera.

SOTTO VOCE *(Italian)*—in a hardly audible undertone.

STRETTO *(Italian)*—a speeding up of tempo at the end of a piece of music for greater dramatic effect. Generally utilized in finales of scenes or acts.

TERZETTO *(Italian)*—a piece for three singers. Synonymous with trio.

TESSITURA *(Italian)*—the general position of the notes in a vocal number. A majority of high notes mean that the aria has a high *tessitura*, a majority of low notes, a low *tessitura*. *Tessi-*

tura is quite distinct from the *range* of a piece which encompasses all notes, from the lowest to the highest.

TREMOLO *(Italian)*—in singing, the rapid repetition of one note, a very difficult feat. Not to be confused with a wavering of pitch.

VIBRATO *(Italian)*—a slight fluctuation of pitch about a single tone, often deliberate. It can be very effective when skillfully done and carefully controlled, but can have a comic effect when exaggerated, and can seem sour when badly done.

Voices are not listed alphabetically, but rather in the descending order of the scale, beginning with the highest female voice, and concluding with the lowest male voice. These classifications are not rigid, since voices vary greatly in range and intensity.

SOPRANO—the female voice with the highest range. Although the sopranos are divided into more specialized classifications, some singers can sing roles in more than one classification.

COLORATURA SOPRANO—the highest and lightest of sopranos, possessed of great vocal agility. Music for the coloratura is generally ornamented with runs and frills. A famous *coloratura* role is Lucia in *Lucia di Lammermoor;* another is Gilda in *Rigoletto.*

DRAMATIC SOPRANO—a powerful high voice, used in dramatic roles. Among the famous ones are the title role in *La Gioconda* and Leonora in *Il Trovatore.* Bruenhilde in Wagner's *Der Ring des Nibelungen* requires an even more powerful voice than the average dramatic soprano possesses.

LYRIC SOPRANO—a lighter, sweeter voice than the dramatic soprano. Examples are Mimi in *La Bohème,* and Violetta in *La Traviata.*

LYRICO SPINTO—a lyric voice with some of the dramatic quality, strength, and range of the dramatic soprano. A soprano with this kind of voice can sing many roles in both lyric and dramatic repertoires. Two *lyrico spinto* roles are Aïda and Tosca.

MEZZO-SOPRANO—the most common female voice. A *mezzo-soprano* can usually sing most *contralto* roles. One type of mezzo voice, a dramatic mezzo, sings roles like Azucena in *Il Trovatore* and Amneris in *Aïda;* the other, a lighter, more lyrical mezzo sings parts like Cherubino in *The Marriage of Figaro.*

CONTRALTO—normally the lowest female voice. Nowadays, few roles in opera are sung by pure contraltos, the mezzo-soprano often taking contralto as well as mezzo parts. Ulrica in

The Masked Ball and Erda in *Siegfried* are two examples of contralto roles. A *contralto,* because of the limited repertoire, does not often study opera. When she does, she tries to extend her range to that of a mezzo-soprano. See *alto.*

ALTO—the lowest boy's voice before it changes in adolescence. In females, the voice is now called *contralto.* The term was also used for male *castrato* and *falsetto* voices. Music is no longer written for the solo *alto,* although many choruses still contain *alto* parts.

FALSETTO—a male singer's special method of using his voice to achieve a tone of female quality, higher than the normal range of the male vioce. The effect of *falsetto* singing is not a natural one.

COUNTERTENOR—the highest male voice, light and clear, not *falsetto* in nature, with a range reaching into the *alto* register. *Countertenors* do not sing *tenor* roles. Much of the music for the *countertenor* was written in the Baroque period, and even earlier. The *countertenor* is rarely heard on the opera stage.

TENOR—the highest masculine-sounding male voice. Below are listed some of the classifications of the tenor voice. But it should be borne in mind that these classifications are not rigid, and that most tenors' voices encompass several of them.

TENOR ROBUSTO—a powerful tenor, used in dramatic roles. Otello in Verdi's opera of that name, Calaf in *Turandot,* and Manrico in *Il Trovatore* are several examples.

LYRIC TENOR—a very beautiful lyric voice, used in more romantic parts, such as Rudolpho in *La Bohème,* and Pinkerton in *Madama Butterfly.*

HELDEN TENOR—a hero tenor, with an extremely powerful voice, capable of rising above the orchestra, and of singing the Wagnerian hero roles.

BARITONE—the middle register of the male voice. The baritone is also the most common male voice. Escamillo in *Carmen,* Silvio in *Pagliacci,* and the title role of *Simon Boccanegra* are examples.

BASS-BARITONE—a voice that reaches into both the bass and baritone ranges. Scarpia in *Tosca* and Amonasro in *Aïda* are well-known bass-baritone roles.

BASSO—the general classification for the lowest male voice. Don Giovanni and Boris Godunov are two great basso roles.

BASSO PROFONDO—the very lowest male voice, as Sarastro in *The Magic Flute.*

acknowledgments

We wish to acknowledge our thanks to the many people who were kind enough to interrupt their extremely busy schedules to answer many questions.

First of all, we want to express our gratitude to the management of the Metropolitan Opera Association, who permitted us to attend rehearsals, and to interview members of the executive and artistic staff. Although it would be impossible to list all those who were cooperative, we owe special thanks to Mr. John Gutman and Mr. Michael Manuel.

We are grateful for the cooperation of the Metropolitan Opera Guild and the staff of *Opera News,* and thank Mr. James Browning of Central Opera Service for reading the chapter on Opera in the United States.

We appreciate the helpfulness of Mr. Mark Schubart of the Juilliard School of Music, and of Mr. Sergius Kagen. They gave generously of their time in discussing the voice and its training. Special mention must be made of Miss Margaret Webster who, on a short visit to the United States, found time to discuss the special problems of directing opera.

We also thank the managements of the New York City Opera, the Lyric Opera of Chicago, and the San Francisco Opera for their help.

We owe a debt of gratitude to all the people who read various chapters and made suggestions. At the same time, we wish to make it clear that all opinions expressed are our own, and that any errors which may have found their way into print are also ours alone.

books for further reading

Blum, Daniel C., *Pictorial Treasury of Opera in America,* Grosset and Dunlap, Inc., New York, 1958.

Briggs, Thomas Henry, *Opera and Its Enjoyment,* Bureau of Publications, Teachers College, Columbia University, New York, 1960.

Brockway, Wallace, and Weinstock, Herbert, *The Opera,* Simon & Schuster, Inc., New York, 1941.

Burrows, Gwynne, *Light Opera Productions for School and Community,* Theodore Presser Co., Philadelphia, 1929.

Cross, Milton J., *New Complete Stories of the Great Operas,* Doubleday & Co., New York, 1955.

Graf, Herbert, *The Opera and its Future in America,* W. W. Norton & Company, New York, 1941.

Graf, Herbert, *Opera for the People,* University of Minnesota Press, Minneapolis, 1951.

Grout, Donald Jay, *A Short History of Opera,* Columbia University Press, New York, 1947.

Huber, Louis H., *Producing Opera in the College,* Bureau of Publications, Teachers College, Columbia University, New York, 1956.

Kagen, Sergius, *On Studying Singing,* Rinehart & Company, Inc., 1950.

Kerman, Joseph, *Opera as Drama,* Alfred A. Knopf, Inc., New York, 1956.

Kolodin, Irving, *The Story of the Metropolitan Opera,* Knopf, New York, 1953.

Lehmann, Lilli, *How to Sing,* Macmillan Company, New York, 1952, third revised edition.

Marek, George R., *World Treasury of Grand Opera,* Harper & Bros., Inc., New York, 1957.

METZ, MRS. CHARLES ABERT, and WICKERSHAM, MARGUERITE, *Opera Manual,* Handbook of practical operatic information, Central Opera Service, New York, 1956, first edition.

NEWMAN, ERNEST, *The Wagner Operas,* Knopf, New York, 1949.

NOBLE, HELEN, *Life with the Met,* G. P. Putnam's Sons, New York, 1954.

SHEEAN, VINCENT, *First and Last Love,* Random House, New York, 1956.

TURFERY, COSSAR, and PALMER, KING, *The Musical Production,* a complete guide for amateurs, Pitman, New York, 1953.

Dictionaries and Encyclopedias

Complete Book of the American Musical Theater, by David Ewen, Henry Holt and Company, New York, 1958.

Encyclopedia of the Opera, by David Ewen, A. A. Wyn, Inc., New York, 1955.

Groves Dictionary of Music and Musicians, fifth edition edited by Eric Blom. St. Martin's Press, New York, 1954.

Harvard Dictionary of Music, by Willi Apel, Harvard University Press, Cambridge, Massachusetts, 1961.

International Cyclopedia of Music and Musicians, editor, Oscar Thompson, eighth edition-revised, edited by Nicholas Slonimsky, Dodd, Mead & Company, New York, 1958.

New College Encyclopedia of Music by J. A. Westrup and F. H. Harrison, W. W. Norton & Company, Inc., New York, 1960.

The Oxford Companion to Music, by Percy A. Scholes, Oxford University Press, London, New York, Toronto, 1955.

Periodicals

Musical America, published by Musical Publications, Ltd., 111 West 57th Street, New York 19, N. Y.

The Musical Quarterly, published by G. Schirmer, Inc., 609 5th Ave., New York 17, N. Y.

Opera News, published by the Metropolitan Opera Guild, 654 Madison Ave., New York 21, N. Y.

Central Opera Service Bulletin, sponsored by The National Council of the Metropolitan Opera Association, 147 West 39th Street, New York 18, N. Y.

The Music Magazine (formerly *The Musical Courier*), published by Summy-Birchard Company, 1834 Ridge Avenue, Evanston, Illinois.

index

Printed in U.S.A.

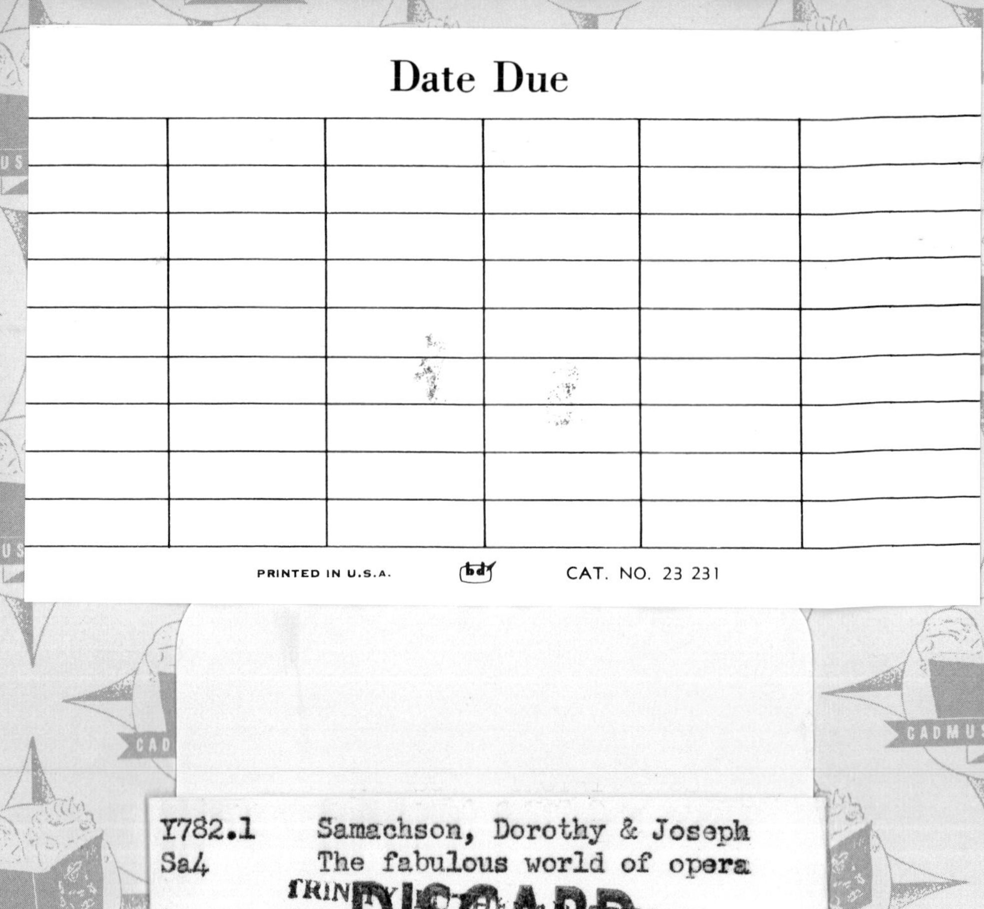
Date Due
PRINTED IN U.S.A.
bd
CAT. NO. 23 231